Kromdraai

Taungs

Cro-Magnon

Neanderthal

THE CASE OF THE MISSING LINK

The Case of the
MISSING LINK

BY

Eleanor Clymer

ILLUSTRATED BY

Robert Reid Macguire

GREAT MYSTERIES
OF SCIENCE

Basic Books, Inc.

Publishers   New York

©1962 by Eleanor Clymer
Library of Congress Catalog Card Number: 62-11585
Printed in the United States of America

For Richard Carvolth

FOREWORD

BY LOREN EISELEY

I am writing this introduction in a remote fishing village on the California coast. Half-wild dogs race in and out of the surf, chasing gulls and sandpipers. From the cliff where I sit, I can see a whale spouting miles offshore. Here man, for all his modern inventions, is still strangely neolithic. He burns the wood cast up on the beach. He is concerned only with fish and fogs and weather. He lives among the elements like his dogs. Like his dogs, also, he occasionally disappears without trace.

Along the wilder coasts of the world, man may thus be occasionally glimpsed as he once was — a part of the earth's great store of living creatures, more cunning than some, yet held to his own place: a little cove by the endless waters. The fisherman holds his thought close to himself; he is suspicious of strangers. Their words are not his words. Here man lives without history. He does not know how he came here.

All of man's civilized accomplishments — his cities, his

libraries and laboratories — rest upon foundations that we can still see in a place like this. Just as the gnarled trees on my cliff sometimes show their roots, groping downward among boulders and crevices, so man today, wherever he lives close to nature, reveals upon what roots his life still depends.

When we read Eleanor Clymer's story of the search for our ancestors, we should remember that it is not a tale involving only our ancestors, interesting though they may be. It is a history that boys and girls relive in every generation, without ever guessing what they are doing.

They have obscure impulses to build tree houses and to hide among the branches from ground-dwelling parents. They are drawn to ponds and fishy streams. They are as sharp-eyed to see a snake or a frog as the men of the world's first dawn. In the pockets of boys, fond mothers find all sorts of mysterious stones and animals. In some children the tree house phase gives way to the dark attraction of caves. In my neighborhood, we boys used to steal away to huge clay banks where we tried, and sometimes succeeded, in boring out shelters like those of cave men.

Children live each day in the marvelous youth of the world that our ancestors knew. If it was a harsh world, it also contained all the wonder, all the mystery that belongs to youth. The child who knows a little of why he loves to swing from a branch, or feels himself drawn by the dark mouths of caves, is learning man's history — not from books but from feelings and emotions, which will grow dimmer with age. If he learns of his past while he still carries it hidden ever so slightly below the surface of his mind, he will enjoy it more.

It is this task that Miss Clymer's book so ably performs, just as I, in imagination, live for a moment among the fishers and their dogs in a time when the world was young. The world for children, and even for a few adults, is only as old as they make it. So here let us re-enter the Age of Stone.

Cave Drawings of Prehistoric Man

CONTENTS

WADJAK

1

THE MISSING ANCESTORS

Have you ever read the mystery about the poor orphan who set out to find out who his parents were? In this old story (which is told in various forms differing in details), the boy begins his search with a definite clue: sometimes it is a ring found in the basket in which he was left on the doorstep of the orphanage; sometimes it is an old letter that mentions the name of a distant Scottish castle. Anyway, the hero starts off, and after many adventures he ends up as the long-lost heir to the manor, or the son of a famous flier, or something like that, and it all ends happily.

The story I am going to tell is also a mystery about a search for ancestors. Whose ancestors? Yours and mine!

The great thing about this story is that it is true. There are many detectives at work on the case, and the clues are scattered all over the world. Often the clues are found buried deep in the earth. The detectives work long hours, sometimes years, hunting for the clues and figuring out what they mean. They don't do it to find a fortune, but simply to discover the answer to an

1

old question that fascinates all of us. And what a thrill it is when they suddenly find a piece to fill out the puzzle!

For instance, in 1891 a young man was digging on the banks of the Solo River in far-away Java. He had come all the way from Holland just to dig there in the mud. Suddenly he saw something so wonderful he could hardly believe his eyes.

What was this wonderful thing? Gold? Diamonds? No. It was a little brown piece of bone — the top of a skull. It had been buried in the earth for thousands and thousands of years,

Dubois   Skull and Head of Early Man (Pithecanthropus)

and had turned to stone. In that way the bone had been preserved, and now this young man, whose name was Eugene Dubois, had been lucky enough to find it. Why did he want to find it? What was he looking for? He was searching for the ancestors of the human race, and this skull cap was a clue.

But why should he have been looking for ancestors? Well, people have always wondered how this world came to be, and where living things came from. Most fascinating of all: Where did Man come from?

Man is so different from all other animals. He is the only mammal that walks upright on two feet, with his head erect. He has a special kind of hand that can handle tools and do all

2

kinds of work. And he has a very special brain. It is more complicated than any other brain, and it is this brain that makes Man so interesting. With it he figures out how to do everything the other animals can do, and more. He makes tools to take the place of claws and sharp teeth. He makes clothes to take the place of fur. He uses fire to warm himself, to cook his food, and to run his machines. He is the only animal who makes paintings and sculptures and composes music. Most important of all, he has language. He talks with his fellow men and shares their ideas. He writes things down in permanent form to be read long after he is dead. In this way knowledge is passed on from generation to generation, and as time goes on the amount of human knowledge grows and grows.

Man is undoubtedly the only animal who looks at himself and wonders, "Where did I come from?"

In early times people invented all sorts of stories about how Man first appeared on the Earth. The ancient Greeks thought that one of their gods, named Prometheus, created the first man. According to the story, one day Prometheus was sitting on the seashore resting, and for amusement he scooped up a handful of wet sand and made a figure like himself. When the figure hardened and dried, it became alive. Its eyes turned blue, its hair golden, and its lips red. Prometheus called it Man:

Pithecanthropus
Leg Bone

He asked his brother Epimetheus to give it some especially nice gift. Prometheus and his brother were in charge of all the animals, and they gave each one a gift. But Epimetheus sadly shook his head. He had just given away the last gift. It was a long neck which he had presented to the giraffe so that it could reach the tall trees. So Prometheus went up to heaven to find something belonging to the gods there. As he passed the sun, he dipped a torch into it and flew quickly back to earth. He gave the burning torch to Man. This, says the Greek story, is the way Man got fire, the most valuable gift in the world.

Some of the American Indians had another idea about how Man was made. They said that the Great Spirit got tired of

3

looking at the barren world, covered with water. He asked the muskrat to dive down to the bottom of the sea and bring up a little mud. Out of the mud he made the Earth. Then he made a woman to live on the Earth, and her children became the ancestors of all people.

The Bible says that Jehovah made the world in six days. He made Man from a bit of clay, and Woman from one of

Primates—the Group to Which Man Also Belongs

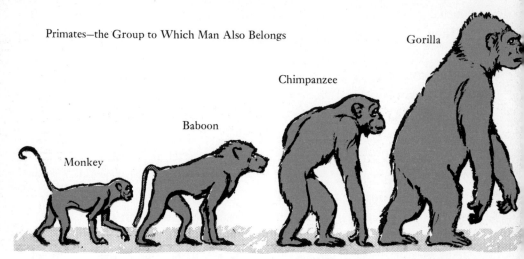

Gorilla

Chimpanzee

Baboon

Monkey

Man's ribs. Their names were Adam and Eve. They lived happily in the Garden of Eden until they ate the fruit of a forbidden tree. Jehovah was so angry that He cast them out of Eden. From that time forth, they had to work hard and earn their bread by the sweat of their brows. They had many children and grandchildren. But some of their descendants finally became so wicked and treated each other so badly that Jehovah decided to make a new start. He sent a great Flood to drown them — all but one good man and his family. The good man was Noah. According to the story, he and his family and the animals they saved in the Ark were the ancestors of all the living things that exist today.

These stories were the attempts of people to explain the miraculous things they saw around them. Before modern science,

4

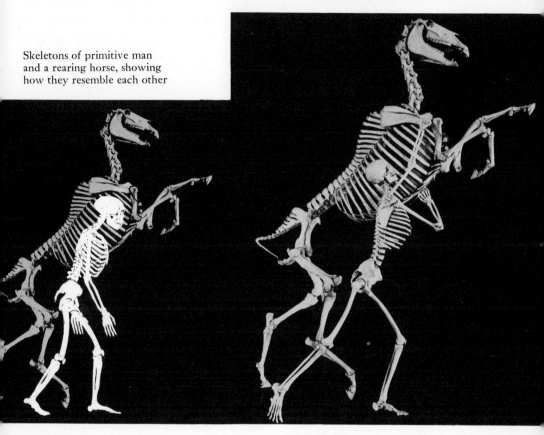

Skeletons of primitive man and a rearing horse, showing how they resemble each other

people had no reliable way of finding the answers to many of their questions, and they merely made up answers by using their imagination. Their myths and legends were often very beautiful and poetic, and they tell us many things about how people felt (and still feel) about nature, about being born and dying, about love and hate and goodness and wickedness.

But people also have an incurable urge to find out how things really happened. In time they discovered facts that contradicted the legends. Scientists began to study living creatures more closely and to hunt for long-dead ones in the earth. They became detectives. They went looking for clues. They used their imaginations too, but with facts as the starting point. And bit by bit, they pieced together a logical picture.

5

2

THE MYSTERIOUS FOSSILS

Back in the Middle Ages, most people in Europe believed that the world and all the creatures in it were created in five days, and that Man was created on the sixth day.

And what was the date of the Creation? Well, it was hard to be sure. But in 1650 Archbishop Ussher, an Irish scholar, figured it out according to the ages of the people mentioned in the Bible. The Creation happened, he said, in 4004 B.C., just about 5,600 years previously. Not long afterward, every living thing perished in the Flood, except Noah and those whom he saved in the Ark. All the animals and people on earth were the descendants of those few individuals.

Fossils of Ancient
Animals and Ferns

Dinosaur Tracks
(right)

Ussher was a very learned man and had read a great many books of history, so his word was believed. Nobody imagined that it was possible to know what had happened *before* there was any written history.

It is true that strange bones had been found from time to time — bones of animals which were no longer seen anywhere. Shells had been found on dry land, and strange teeth, and the prints of leaves, and even the outline of a fish's body or the track made by an animal's foot in the solid rock.

No one knew what kinds of creatures these bones and shells and strange prints belonged to, but people gave them a name. They called them fossils. The name comes from a Latin word meaning "to dig." Some said that the bones were those of giants or dragons. The prints of fish and leaves and the stony shells and teeth were explained as "freaks of nature." Some chemical action was supposed to have made the rocks *look* like animals or plants.

Now, of course, we know that fossils really are the remains of animals or plants that lived many thousands or even millions

HOW A FISH BECAME A FOSSIL

It lived in an ancient sea

It died and sank to the bottom

Layers of mud buried it

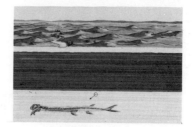
The sea dried up

of years ago. Usually when a living thing dies, it decays and disappears. But sometimes something happens to preserve it. Bones may be buried by mud that hardens to rock. The mud seeps into the tiny spaces inside the bone and turns to rock there, so that the whole bone seems to be made of stone. Sometimes the soft parts of an animal leave a print in the mud before they decay. Then the mud hardens to stone. Sometimes bones are preserved in the dry air of a desert. And there have even been discoveries of animals buried for centuries in ice, which preserved them so well that they still had their hair and flesh!

But back in the Middle Ages all of this was unknown. Most people firmly believed that no type of animal or plant had died out since Noah, and no new ones had been created.

However, explorers kept turning up more and more strange creatures. When America was discovered, new birds and beasts were found — different from those in Europe, yet also like them in many ways. How had they come into existence? People began to wonder if, after all, the history of life on the earth might be more complicated than they had thought.

Curiosity is a funny thing. It is catching. Here and there, little by little, more people began to explore, even if it was only in their own back yards. More people got interested in digging

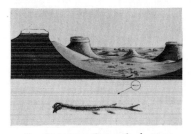
Erosion wore down the layers

Finally the fossil fish was dug up

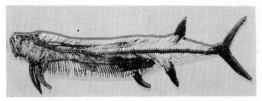
The little fish it had swallowed was still in its stomach

8

and in observing nature. It became harder to be satisfied with the old explanations.

John Ray, an English parson and naturalist, who lived from 1627 to 1705, was a fine observer. In 1663 he studied an old forest which had been buried under the sea at one time and had turned to rock; now the sea had dried up and the petrified forest was exposed on dry land. He noticed other layers of deposits which had accumulated on what was once the sea bottom. Seeing how slowly things changed in a man's lifetime, Ray thought that it must have taken a very long time for these layers of rock and mountains and other features of the landscape to develop. He couldn't help feeling that the world must be a great deal older than most people thought.

John Ray

He looked at fossil leaf prints and thought: "If these are the remains of real leaves, how long it must have taken to make them!"

But he didn't quite dare admit that it might have taken longer than 6,000 years, for this would mean contradicting the Bible.

The first man to propose a scientific theory about the history of the Earth was James Hutton, a Scottish physician. He asked how it was that different layers of rock were piled one on another, with different kinds of fossils in them. If there had been only one Creation and one Flood, this was hard to understand. Some people tried to explain it by saying that maybe there were several creations and floods, and each layer, with its fossils, represented a period that was ended by a flood. But Hutton said it wasn't like that at all. He said that the only way to explain the history of the Earth was to observe what was still going on.

James Hutton

He had been observing a river near his home. He saw how it carried bits of clay and mud down to the sea. He said that all the rivers of the world had been doing this for thousands and thousands of years. In this way layers of deposits had

been built up on the bottom of seas. Gradually they had hardened into rock. When seas dried up, the rock was slowly worn away again by water. There had been no series of catastrophes. Instead, the layers had been formed and eroded by the same kind of very slow processes that were still going on. So the Earth and everything in it must be much older than anybody had imagined.

William Smith

Count Buffon

Baron Cuvier

Hutton published a book in 1795, called *Theory of the Earth*, but no one paid much attention to it.

A few years later, William Smith, an engineer and surveyor, worked out a system of geology. Smith knew a great deal about the land of England. Many canals were being built, and he had laid out canal routes, had dug in coal fields and swamps, and had found many fossils. He saw that it was possible to classify rocks according to the fossils found in them. If the same kind of fossil was found in certain rocks in different places in the earth, one could be sure these rocks were of about the same age. One could also be sure they were very old.

A French scientist named Count Buffon had also argued that the Earth was quite old. He thought it had been red-hot in the beginning and had taken 70,000 years to cool off enough for life to exist. (We know now that the Earth is much, much older.) Buffon wrote a book in 1749, called *Natural History*, in which he said that living things changed from age to age, and that some animals had become extinct because the Earth had become too cool for them.

And so, people gradually came to see that the Earth must be more than 6,000 years old, and that the fossils in it were really the remains of ancient creatures which had disappeared from the living world.

A French scientist, Baron Cuvier, who lived from 1769 to 1832, studied all the fossils he could find. He knew so much about the anatomy of living creatures that he could figure out how an ancient animal must have looked from just a few bones.

But what about Man? Where did he fit into the picture? Most people said that he had been created separately, at the time of the last great Creation. Cuvier agreed with this idea and said firmly that no such thing as a human fossil would be found.

Still, there were some signs of early Man in the rocks. Ever since the days of the ancient Greeks, people had been finding stone tools in the ground. These were thought to be thunderbolts which fell from the sky during storms. The fact that nobody had ever actually seen a stone axe fall from the sky didn't bother the people who held this theory.

A few people insisted that the ancient stone tools must have been made by men. But most people could not believe that men had ever been so barbarous as to use chipped stone tools. Why make them of stone when iron was so much better?

When the discoverers of America found that the Indians

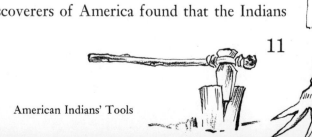

11

American Indians' Tools

Elephant in Roman England

had stone tools, people still maintained that the Indians must be a once civilized race which had "degenerated" into barbarism!

But there were questions, questions, and more questions. Diggers found stone tools buried deep in the earth, in strata (or layers) that had been laid down long, long before the supposed dates of the Creation of man or of Noah's Flood. Could there have been men on the earth in those days? Impossible, said the interpreters of the Bible.

In 1715 a London pharmacist named Conyers, looking around in British soil for old bones and ivory, which were sometimes used for medicine, found what looked like the skeleton of an elephant, and near it a chipped flint. This certainly was mysterious, because there were no elephants in England. But a friend of his came to the rescue with what sounded like a reasonable explanation: the elephant must have been brought to England by Roman soldiers in the time of the Emperor Claudius, and probably a native Briton had killed it with the flint spearhead.

In 1771 a German, Johann Esper, found some *human bones* at the same level as those of extinct animals. This was really upsetting. How had they got there? Esper didn't dare to say that they belonged to an "antediluvian" man, one who had lived before Noah's Flood. He decided the human bones must have got into this rock level by some kind of accident.

In 1797 John Frere, an Englishman, found some flint axes and other tools buried 13 feet deep with the bones of large, extinct animals. He was sure they belonged to "a very distant period, much more remote in time than the modern world." But this, too, was ignored.

12

William Buckland, a teacher of geology at Oxford, found human skeletons buried in caves in Wales and England. But he simply refused to believe that they dated back before the Flood. He said the caves had been used as burial places and that was why the bones had been buried so deep. The fact that there were stone tools with these bones, and that there was no sign of anyone having dug into the rock floor of the caves before he got there, was conveniently disregarded.

We might ask why these people refused to see something that was right in front of their noses. The answer is that it is very hard to make people believe something they don't want to believe. When you have been taught from your earliest childhood that certain things are true, it is hard to believe that they may not be. For thousands of years people thought, for instance, that the world was flat, and that the sun revolved around the earth. When scientists told them it was just the other way around, they were very upset about it. It took a long time to convince them.

In the same way it was hard to convince the public that Man might have been on earth longer than 6,000 years. It was hard to convince even scientists.

In 1823 Baron Cuvier was shown a human skeleton which had been found in some ancient mud with remains of extinct animals. He wouldn't have anything to do with it. He said that, as far as he knew, there weren't any human fossils dating back before the last upheavals of the Earth.

Perhaps Cuvier shouldn't be blamed too much for saying this. People had sent him bones from all over Europe, which they claimed came from antediluvian man, and most of them had turned out to be animal bones. Some were human, to be sure, but there was no accurate information about where they had come from, so Cuvier couldn't really say how old they were.

But more evidence was coming in all the time.

13

Stone-Age Tools Found by Boucher de Perthes

A French lawyer named Edouard Lartet became interested in paleontology, the study of life in past ages. Lartet went exploring in his own district of Sansan in France. There he found the jaws and teeth of a fossil ape, which he named Pliopithecus, meaning Pliocene Ape. Later he found another jaw, which he called Dryopithecus, meaning Forest Ape. This was encouraging. If fossil apes could be found, why not Man?

Another Frenchman, Jacques Boucher de Perthes, was doing his best to prove that remains of ancient man could be found in Europe. Boucher de Perthes lived from 1788 to 1868. He worked as a customs official in Abbeville. He liked to walk along the Somme Canal and watch the men dredging there. In the mud and stones dug up by the dredges, he found fossil bones and stone tools. This aroused his interest in archaeology (the study of cities, buildings, tools, and other things left by early peoples).

Boucher de Perthes was sure that the chipped stones he had found meant early man had lived in the neighborhood. He visited quarries and poked about among beds of gravel which had once been river beds. Wherever he went, he found stone axes. At last he had a tremendous collection. He exhibited the tools before the learned scientists of France to prove that Stone Age Man had existed. He wrote a book about his discoveries. To his surprise, nobody believed his theories. They said that the stones had become chipped by accident, and that Boucher de Perthes was somewhat crazy.

But he refused to be discouraged. He kept on working and writing. At last, in 1858, several English scientists went to visit him and see his collections. There were the tools he had found among the bones of extinct mammoths (elephant-like animals) and rhinoceroses. They went to the gravel beds to see for themselves. There was a stone axe in an undisturbed bed of gravel, eleven feet below the surface of the ground. They were convinced that Boucher de Perthes was right. These things had been made and used by men who lived many ages ago.

14

In 1859 this information was presented at a meeting of the Royal Society in London. All of the most famous scientists were there. One of Boucher de Perthes' friends read a paper about his findings. At last the scientific world (with a few exceptions) was convinced. Boucher de Perthes, John Frere, and the others who had suspected the truth were right. Not only was the world older than anybody had imagined, but so was Man.

Nor did the matter rest there. More startling discoveries were being made. In 1858, an Englishman named Charles Darwin astounded everybody with a new theory about how living things had developed on the Earth.

Prehistoric Mammoth and Rhinoceros

THE ORIGIN OF SPECIES 3

Charles Darwin was born in 1809. He grew up in a house with a beautiful garden in the English countryside. Like most boys and girls, Charles liked to collect things. In his case, he went off on collecting expeditions partly to get away from school, which he found terribly boring. The school taught almost nothing but Latin and Greek. Charles' father, a well-to-do doctor, wanted him to be educated as a gentleman. Charles did his best to please his father. But he just could not get interested in Latin and Greek.

What *did* interest him was bugs. Bugs and birds and flowers, and all the fascinating things that he found when he went for a walk. Charles would let his school work go and spend his time in the woods and fields collecting plants and animals. He also did chemical experiments with his brother in a shed in the garden.

This was not unusual. It was the style in those days to make a hobby of natural science. But Charles' father thought he was spending altogether too much time on this sort of thing. It kept the boy from studying Latin and Greek, which were supposed to be the best subjects to develop the mind.

In spite of his father's objections, Charles became more and more interested in nature. He also liked to go hunting. Anything to be outdoors. It got to the point where his father said angrily: "You care for nothing but shooting, dogs, and rat-catching, and will be a disgrace to yourself and all your family."

The headmaster of his school did not approve of Charles' chemical experiments. He said: "This stupid fellow will attend to his gases and his rubbish, yet will not work at anything really useful."

Charles was sorry, but science was what appealed to him most. Nowadays a boy who has so much interest in science usually becomes a scientist. His family and friends do all they can to encourage him. But Dr. Darwin considered science just a hobby for one's spare time — not a subject for a man to devote his whole life to.

Still, in order to make use of what Charles had managed to learn, it was decided he should be a doctor. He was sent to the University of Edinburgh in Scotland. But medicine, too, bored

University of Edinburgh

Charles. He refused to study it and came home. Now what was to be done with him?

There seemed to be no use trying to make him go into the army or the navy or the law. The only thing left was to be a minister. Those were the only kinds of work that a gentleman's son could do. Charles said that would be all right if he could be a *country* minister. Then he could keep on going for walks and collecting things in his spare time.

At 19, Charles went to Cambridge University to learn to be a minister. In his spare time he studied botany and zoology.

He met other men who were interested in natural science. To-gether they went on field trips with their teachers to explore the countryside. Darwin's best friend among his teachers was the Reverend Henslow. Reverend Henslow taught mathematics and theology, but he was also interested in botany, chemistry, geology, and entomology and had worked with a famous geol-ogist named Adam Sedgwick. Today we would not consider this enough training for teaching science at a university, but in those days teachers often knew little more about science than their students.

Darwin read all the books he could find and talked with as many people as possible. He went digging for fossils with Pro-fessor Sedgwick and insect-hunting with Reverend Henslow. He became more and more excited about his scientific pursuits. He was learning to be a very good observer, and an honest ob-server. That is, he took note of what he saw, and did not try to see anything that wasn't there.

Now the time had come for him to graduate and to get a job as a minister. But just at that moment he received an excit-ing offer. A ship, *H.M.S. Beagle*, was about to set sail on a voyage around the world. It would carry men and instruments

The *Beagle's* Route Around the World

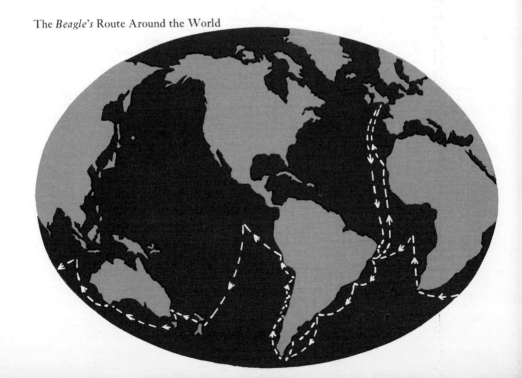

to chart the oceans, and the captain wanted a naturalist to go along to gather useful information. Reverend Henslow was offered the job, but he could not go. He recommended Charles Darwin instead.

What a wonderful chance to see the world and learn about the strange and interesting things in it! Charles was almost prevented from getting this chance, because his father opposed the trip, on the ground that it would only make the young man more shiftless. But his uncle persuaded Dr. Darwin that it wouldn't do any real harm. So off Charles sailed. It was five years before he came home again.

Those five years were to have tremendous results, not only for Charles, but for the whole science of biology.

Charles had always been a collector. Now he had the whole world to collect in. Every time the ship stopped, he went ashore and brought back boatloads of specimens: plants, insects, rocks, bones, shells. His shipmates said he would sink the ship with this junk. The captain was none too pleased. Charles was not getting the kind of useful information he had in mind. He wanted to know where to find gold and silver.

H.M.S. Beagle in the Straits of Magellan

But Darwin kept on. He took side trips into the mountains and jungles. He kept records of everything he learned. At college he had been taught to classify living things into orders, families, and species. Now, as he classified his specimens, he learned some very remarkable things.

In Europe there was a species of fungus that had a peculiar odor. Darwin found the same species in South America. And he also found there the same special kind of beetle that lived on this fungus.

In Siberia and in Brazil there were certain worms that lived in the sand at the edges of salt lakes. In both places, the same kinds of birds came to feed on them.

Darwin began to wonder. Was there a special reason why the same kinds of animals and plants turned up in the same kind of living place?

Then he noticed something else. Turtles in America were much like turtles in Europe and they seemed to be closely related, yet there were differences between the species in size, color, and ways of life. The same was true of lizards in Europe and America. What caused these differences?

Furthermore, what about the animals that had become extinct? What had made these animals die out?

All these questions and many more had to be answered. After Darwin returned home, he got to work studying his notes and his collections of specimens. He read and re-read the books of other scientists. Finally he came to a strange conclusion. His idea was so radical that for a long time he was afraid to publish it. He wanted to be sure he was right. He let 22 years go by before he published his findings. Even then he might not have done so if another man by the name of Alfred Wallace had not come to the same conclusion. This is something that often happens in science. Usually an idea blossoms in several places at once.

Anyway, Darwin's friends persuaded him that it was time to announce his findings, and his paper and Wallace's were pub-

20

lished at the same time, in 1858. Darwin's book was called *The Origin of Species*. It answered the questions he had been asking.

First, there was the question: Why are living things different from one another? For instance, how did some turtles get to be bigger, or differently colored, or thicker-shelled than other turtles?

Darwin's answer went like this: In any environment, there is only a certain amount of food and space. The animals (or plants) living there compete with one another for these necessities of life. This fight is called the Struggle for Existence. It is carried on in many ways. The trees that grow taller than those around them get more sunlight; those that grow longer roots reach more water in the ground. Likewise, animals that have stronger teeth and claws than their rivals can eat the weaker ones. Animals with swift legs can run away from their enemies. Those with teeth suited for chewing grass can live off the grass of the field. And so it goes. Everywhere the creatures that happen to be better fitted to find food and defend themselves survive, while those less fitted die young, usually before they have grown old enough to bear offspring.

So the stronger, the swifter, the better-adapted animals or plants produce more descendants. These descendants tend to have the same superior gifts that their parents had — a tall habit of growth (if they are trees in the jungle), or sharp teeth and

claws (if they are tigers), or speed of foot, or whatever helps them to make a living in their environment. This is called Survival of the Fittest. It is also called Natural Selection, because it is nature's way of selecting those that will survive.

In this way, over a long period, animals and plants change and new species arise. This is the secret of the "origin of species." They arise in response to the conditions of the environment. This is why we find big white bears in some places and small black bears in others. This is why we find some birds with short, strong beaks for cracking seeds, and other birds with long, thin beaks for picking insects out of holes or sipping nectar from flowers. Animals and plants adapt themselves to the places where they live. And since those places are different, the animals and plants become different too, in the course of long centuries.

Living places also change. The climate may get colder or warmer or drier or wetter. Then the plants or animals that were adapted to the old climate may die. But a few of them may be a little different from their parents. They may have just the difference needed to survive. Some bears may have thicker fur coats. Ordinarily this may not be important. But when the temperature drops suddenly, the bears with the thicker coats are better able to stand the cold. Then they have the best chance of growing up and bearing young. And the same is true of their offspring: those with the thickest coats are the most likely to reproduce themselves. In this way the surviving breed of bears gradually develops a thicker and thicker coat. Eventually it becomes so different from its ancestors that it has to be considered a new species.

That, said Darwin, explains how different species of bears and turtles and birds and other animals come into being. It also explains why they are alike in many ways—they come from the same ancestors!

Darwin called the process *evolution*. Species change when conditions change. The ones that cannot change die out.

Here at last was the answer to the mystery of the fossils — the strange animals that could no longer be found among the living creatures of the earth. They had become extinct because they could not adapt to new conditions.

Why had Darwin been so afraid to publish his theory? Why had he waited 22 years to tell the world about it? The reason is that he knew there would be violent objections and he wanted to be sure he was right. We must remember that when he went off in the *Beagle*, he himself still thought that species were fixed, just as they had been created.

Of course people knew that it was possible to change animals and plants. After all, farmers had been breeding cattle and raising vegetables for many years. But most people still didn't think that these things happened in nature. They still didn't want to believe that the horses and cows they knew had descended from forms which were very different. They couldn't give up the age-old idea of original Creation. When Darwin published his book, he himself was a bit frightened. "It is like confessing a murder," he wrote to a friend. Darwin *had* committed a murder — of cherished ideas.

Those who were shocked by his theory were soon to get an even worse shock.

What about Man? Did Darwin think that Man himself was a product of evolution? Yes, he did think it might be possible. He suggested that all animals, including Man, probably were descended from common ancestors.

Darwin discussed this idea in another book, *The Descent of Man*, which he published in 1871. In that book he concluded that Man was indeed descended from some earlier form of life.

Everybody knows that Man and the apes are very much alike. They are classified as belonging to the same family — the primates. Monkeys are like funny imitations of people. That's why we like to look at them in the zoo. But Man is like other animals, too. His skeleton can be compared with that of any other mammal. His muscles and heart, brain and blood vessels are like those of other mammals.

Even more remarkable, the human embryo — the baby before it is born — looks like the embryos of other animals. At one point the human embryo has a tail, and even gill slits like those of a fish! These features fade away as the embryo develops, and they have disappeared by the time the baby is born.

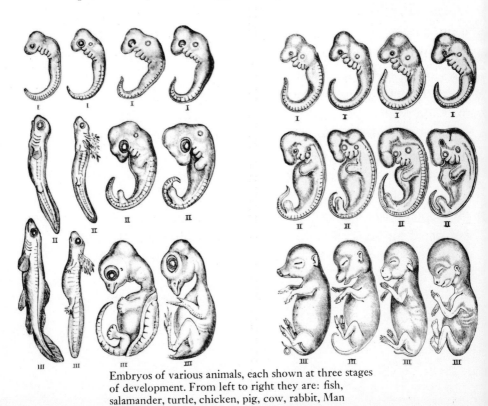

Embryos of various animals, each shown at three stages of development. From left to right they are: fish, salamander, turtle, chicken, pig, cow, rabbit, Man

The human baby still has some leftover things it doesn't need, such as the appendix and the muscles that can move the ears. In Man these are useless, but in some of the lower animals they serve a useful purpose. So here is further evidence that Man is related to the lower animals.

Because Man and the apes were plainly alike in many ways, Darwin thought that the differences between Man and the apes could be accounted for by Natural Selection.

The uproar was tremendous. Man, the ruler of the world, descended from a common ancestor with the monkeys! Ridiculous! What about Man's brain? What about his feelings?

Darwin admitted that there was a great difference between the brain power of the highest ape and the lowest savage. But, he said, there is an even greater difference between a fish and an ape. He argued that by countless tiny steps an ape-like ancestor could have evolved into Man. The differences between Man and many animals were differences of degree, not of kind.

Animals apparently feel pleasure, pain, love, and fear, as Man does. Dogs have good memories. Monkeys are curious and intelligent and can learn many tricks. They can even reason.

Darwin liked to tell the story of a female baboon which stole puppies and kittens and raised them in a very loving way. One day a kitten scratched her. The baboon was surprised. She looked at the kitten's feet, and then nipped off its claws!

But people couldn't accept the idea that Man had come from a monkey-like creature. "Prove it!" they said.

"Where is the missing link? Where are the fossils of Man's ancestors?"

Darwin couldn't answer that. He could only say that some day missing links would be found. He thought they might be found in Africa, because that was where the gorillas and chimpanzees still lived. More than that he couldn't say.

But geologists — scientists who study the Earth and its rocks — soon found plenty of proof that Darwin's ideas about the evolution of life were correct.

HISTORY IN THE ROCKS 4

The father of modern geology was William Smith. Remember that we met him in the chapter before last. Born 40 years before Darwin, Smith was the English engineer and canal builder who first identified the layers of the Earth's rocks by the fossils they contained. He pointed out that each layer must represent a different period in the Earth's history.

James Hutton was right in his idea about how these layers, or strata, were formed. Originally they were deposits of dust, sand, gravel, and mud, laid down by running water and the wind. Over millions of years, as climates changed and the seas rose and fell, layer was piled on layer. In the course of time the strata hardened into rock.

Today we can see the strata clearly wherever rivers have cut into the rock. We also see them when we dig into hillsides or deep into the earth to build canals, roads, or mines. In places like the Grand Canyon of Colorado the strata look like a layer cake, each layer a different color from the others.

After Darwin proposed his theory about how life evolved, paleontologists went hunting in the strata to see what fossils they could find. Each layer should be older than the one above

26

Exposed Strata in the Grand Canyon

it. As they went down to deeper layers, they should find older and older animals and plants. In this way they might piece together a picture of the history of life on the Earth.

The paleontologists found that sometimes the same kind of fossil would turn up in many different parts of the world. This was very convenient, because it helped them to check their findings. For instance, if a certain kind of fossil fish was found in a layer of rock in England and in a layer of rock in France, they knew that the two layers were of the same age.

Of course, they rarely found a complete set of layers in any one place showing all the periods. The action of winds and rivers and rains varies from region to region. Then, too, earthquakes break up the earth; mountains rise up and push the layers out of place; or parts of the Earth's crust slip so that the layers no longer match. But the geologists learned how to recognize the kinds of strata wherever they found them.

Here is the fascinating story of the Earth's history as scientists now read it from the rocks. They divide it into four great chapters, or eras, each millions of years long.

The first and longest was the Archaean Era. Archaean means very old. It goes back to the beginning of the Earth.

During that time the basic rocks solidified from the original hot mass. The oceans were formed from the rain that poured down on the young Earth as it cooled.

Life began some time during the Archaean Era. We are not sure just when or where the first living things were formed, but some of the fossils of algae that have been found seem to be two billion years old!

After the Archaean came the Paleozoic Era (era of ancient life); the Mesozoic (era of middle life); and the Cenozoic (era of recent life).

Each era has been divided into periods. The periods are usually named for the places where they were first studied. For instance, the first period of the Paleozoic is called Cambrian, because Cambria is a name for Wales and it was in Wales that these rocks were first studied by Adam Sedgwick.

Far, far down in the rocks, at the beginning of the Paleozoic, we find traces of ancient seaweeds and worms in what was once soft mud. A little higher up there are remains of trilobites, the ancestors of horseshoe crabs. With them are scallop-like, double-shelled animals called brachiopods; jellyfish and sea lilies; and many more sea animals without backbones.

Still higher come the primitive jawless fishes, the first animals with backbones. They were strange looking creatures, covered with heavy bony plates to protect them from their enemies. They could not swim much; they could only grub about in the mud of the ancient seas for their food. But their descendants developed jaws and fins and learned to swim about and catch their prey.

In a thick layer of red sandstone, geologists have found the fossils of so many kinds of fishes that they refer to that time as the Age of Fishes. The period of red sandstone is called the Devonian, because it was first studied in Devon, England.

After the Devonian came the Carboniferous period, when huge ferns and palm trees grew in the steamy swamps all over the world. They died and eventually turned into coal.

28

Time Scale	ERAS	Duration of periods	PERIODS	DOMINANT ANIMAL LIFE
			Recent	Man
0 10 20 30 40 50 60	**CENOZOIC** 60 million years duration	60	Pleistocene Pliocene Miocene Oligocene Eocene Paleocene	Mammals
70 80 90 100	**MESOZOIC** 140 million years duration	60	Cretaceous	Dinosaurs
150		35	Jurassic	
200		45	Triassic	
	PALEOZOIC 350 million years duration	25	Permian	Primitive reptiles
250		20	Pennsylvanian	
		30	Mississippian	Amphibians
300		65	Devonian	
350		35	Silurian	Fishes
400		75	Ordovician	Invertebrates
450 500		90	Cambrian	

PROTEROZOIC

ARCHAEOZOIC

1500 MILLION YEARS DURATION

BEGINNINGS OF LIFE

Toward the end of the Paleozoic there were droughts. As pools or rivers dried up, some of the ancient fishes managed to slide over land to reach the remaining pools. Those fishes that could move over land had descendants which could stay out of water even longer. They developed into amphibians, meaning animals that can live both in water and on land. Amphibians have lungs and can breathe air. But their eggs must be laid in water, and the young must live in the water until their legs grow out.

One fine day some of the amphibians' descendants found they could stay out of water altogether. The Age of Reptiles had arrived. This was the Mesozoic Era, which has three periods: the Triassic, Jurassic, and Cretaceous. Cretaceous means chalky, and this was the time when the chalk cliffs of England were built up from the tiny white shells of incredible numbers of little creatures, some no bigger than the head of a pin!

During the Mesozoic Era, huge reptiles ruled the Earth. They developed into the dinosaurs, plesiosaurs, and other monsters. They had cold blood and very small brains, and they laid hard-shelled eggs.

Early Amphibian

Then suddenly most of the reptiles died out, leaving only the few smaller descendants, such as lizards, snakes, and crocodiles, that we see today. Probably the great reptiles died because the climate turned colder as the Mesozoic ended and the Cenozoic began. They could not stand cold weather.

But another kind of creature could.

During the Mesozoic a family of small animals had developed from a side branch of the reptile family. The new creatures were mammals. When the bigger reptiles disappeared, the mammals took over, like distant cousins inheriting the estate when all the high chieftains have fallen by the wayside.

The mammals developed warm blood and fur or hair to keep them warm. They had a better system of reproduction. Most important of all, they had better brains.

The birds also had their start during the Mesozoic. They, too, had warm blood, were protected by feathers, and could live through cold weather.

Now came the Cenozoic Era. It is divided into six periods: Paleocene, Eocene, Oligocene, Miocene, Pliocene, and Pleistocene. All kinds of mammals appeared as the Cenozoic proceeded. There were big creatures like the dinotherium, the ancestor of the elephant; little ones like the hyracotherium, the small ancestor of the horse; and a special group that gave rise to the first primates.

At the beginning of the Cenozoic, about 75 million years ago, there were some little animals, about the size of a mouse, that lived in trees and fed on insects. We know them from a few tiny skulls and primate-like teeth. Some of them developed into creatures with larger brains, shorter snouts, and feet like hands, with nails instead of claws. Some looked like modern tarsiers and lemurs, only larger.

First Feathered
Bird

For millions of years these early primates developed and spread over most of the world, until, in the Oligocene, one branch of the family became the earliest monkeys. It is true we know these monkeys only from one lower jaw. But even so, anatomists can say pretty confidently that the creature was about the size of a squirrel. We call it Parapithecus. Possibly this monkey was an ancestor of ours!

In the next period, the Miocene, we find the first fossils of apes. One has been found in central Africa, which seems to have been a good place for apes to live. It is called Proconsul. It was a light creature, slender and active. Probably it did not climb trees, as modern apes do, but was good at running on the ground.

From the next period, the Pliocene, fossils of apes have turned up in Europe and other parts of the world. In fact, it seems that anthropoid apes flourished all over Africa, Asia, and Europe during Miocene and Pliocene times. But no apes have been found in America.

And then at last, in the Pleistocene, the Age of Man began.

NEANDERTHAL MAN

In 1856 some workmen in Germany were digging out part of a cliff in a little valley called Neanderthal. There were many ancient limestone caves in this valley.

Limestone is a rather soft, white stone. If you put a little acid on this stone, it bubbles or fizzes, because limestone is alkaline and reacts chemically with the acid. When water from brooks or melting snow runs through limestone, the acids in the water (which come from the soil) gradually wear away the stone. After many years, the waters may make huge holes in the rock. These are limestone caves.

Animals sometimes use caves as shelters, and people have used them, too. They often lived in caves in the early days before they learned how to build houses. Sometimes they died there, and their bones were buried by dust and earth. That is why caves are good places to look for fossils.

The quarrymen who were digging in the Neanderthal were not looking for fossils. They were digging limestone to be used for smelting iron ore in furnaces.

The entrances to the caves were very narrow. To widen them, the workmen blew up part of the rock face. Then they climbed into the first cave. In order to get to the limestone, they had to dig away nearly six feet of earth and rubbish. As they chopped and hacked with their pickaxes, they turned up some old bones. They began to shovel the bones out of the cave. When the pieces of bones tumbled down, the quarry owner shouted: "What are you doing there?"

"Just digging out an old skeleton we found," the men answered.

The quarry owner examined the bones. They were thick and heavy, and he thought they were probably the skeleton of a cave bear.

"Maybe the schoolmaster would like them," he said. So the bones were passed on to Johann Fuhlrott, a science teacher in the local high school, who loved to explore the rocks and had a collection of fossils.

When Fuhlrott saw the bones, he was amazed. These were certainly not from a bear. The skeleton was not complete; there were only the top of the skull, the leg bones, and some bits of arm bones and ribs. But Fuhlrott, who knew a bit about anatomy, was sure they must have belonged to a man.

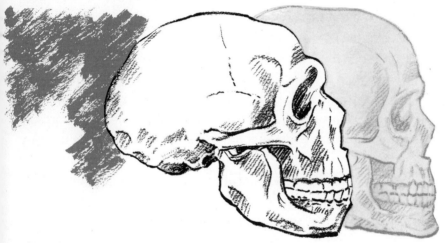

Skulls of Neanderthal (*left*) and Modern Man (*right*)

But what a strange man! The top of the skull was flat. There were heavy ridges over the eye holes, where the eyebrows would have been. The skull bones were thicker than any human ones he had ever seen. The thigh bones were thick and heavy and curved; the creature probably walked with a stooping gait.

Fuhlrott thought that this must be older than any human skeleton ever found before. Could it be the ancestor of Man that the scientists were looking for?

The teacher lost no time in showing the bones to a famous anthropologist, Professor Schaafhausen of Bonn University. The professor agreed that they were probably human. He took

33

Comparison of Skeletons of Neanderthal Man (stooping) and Modern Man (upright)

the precious bones to the university museum, and at the next meeting of natural scientists he announced the find. He invited Fuhlrott to come and address the great men of science.

Were the assembled scientists happy and excited over the discovery? They were not. They thought it was all nonsense. Poor Fuhlrott! Here he was, showing his great discovery to the celebrated scientists who were his idols, and they laughed at him. The great Dr. Rudolf Virchow, who knew more than anybody else about anatomy, said the strange skeleton must have been deformed by some bone disease. Another scientist thought the skull might be the malformed skull of an idiot.

The scientists pointed out that there was no way of knowing how old the bones were. This was true, of course, because the workmen who had found them had not bothered to note what stratum of rock had held them. Besides, no other remains had been found that might date the fossils. Someone suggested that the skeleton might just have been washed into the cave by rain water (overlooking the fact that actually the mouth of the cave was blocked by rock before the workmen blasted it away).

Schaafhausen stuck to his guns. These could not be the bones of any man such as people had ever laid eyes on. They were too much like those of an animal. And yet they did have human features. He insisted that this proved that Man had descended from animal-like ancestors.

Virchow said it proved nothing of the kind. According to all the evidence of other ancient skeletons, he said, the men of the Stone Ages looked no different from modern man. This skeleton, he maintained, was simply that of a man whose thigh bones had been bowed by rickets, whose skull had been flattened by heavy blows, and who had suffered from arthritis in his old age.

The furore over Schaafhausen's proposal about man's descent from animals was tremendous. It was very hard for people to admit that man might once have been so ape-like.

34

One man wrote: "This skeleton may have belonged to one of those wild men, half-crazed, half idiotic, cruel and strong, who . . . now and then appear in civilized communities, to be consigned to the penitentiary or the gallows when their murderous propensities manifest themselves."

In the midst of these discussions, an English scientist remembered that he had found a fossilized skull at Gibraltar in 1848. Nobody had known what to make of it, so it had been put away. Now (in 1864) this skull was brought out and compared with the Neanderthal specimen. Everyone had to agree that they were surprisingly alike!

Scientists and the general public became more and more interested in Neanderthal. Was he really an early man? If he was, what had his ancestors been like? Could a missing link be found which would relate him to the apes?

More exploring went on, and more fossils were found. Some were like Neanderthal; others were almost exactly, if not exactly, like modern man. It was very puzzling. Scientists did not yet fully realize that they were finding different types of prehistoric men who had lived in different periods.

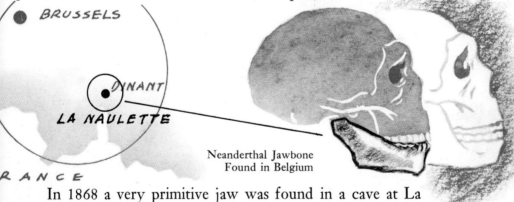

BRUSSELS

DINANT

LA NAULETTE

RANCE

Neanderthal Jawbone
Found in Belgium

In 1868 a very primitive jaw was found in a cave at La Naulette in Belgium. It was the first jawbone that looked as if it belonged to a Neanderthal man (in the skeleton found in the Neanderthal Valley, the jaw was missing). This find now showed that Neanderthal man, if it was indeed *his* jaw, had human teeth.

35

In 1860 Edouard Lartet of France explored a cave in Massat and found many bones, flints, and stone tools. In a heap of rubbish he discovered the antler of a deer with a picture scratched on it — a drawing of a cave bear's head! Only a human being could have made such a drawing. There could not be much doubt that it was an ancient man.

But more dramatic evidence was to come. Four years later Lartet dug up, in ancient soil under a cliff in the Vezere Valley, a mammoth's tusk, and on this tusk was engraved a picture of a mammoth. Now mammoths have long been extinct; here was proof that thinking men, who drew pictures, lived in the long-ago age of the mammoths.

The engraved tusk was shown at the Exhibition in Paris in 1867. Crowds of people came to see the stone tools and the drawings of the cave bear and the mammoth.

The following year an even more exciting discovery turned up. Lartet's son, Louis, went to dig in the same valley in a cave which had been exposed by the building of a railroad. In this cave, called Cro-Magnon, he found a regular museum of human relics — flint tools, carved antlers, shells, and teeth with holes bored in them, as if for stringing in necklaces. And best of all, he dug up skeletons of people who had lived in this cave.

Among the remains were the bones of four men, a woman, and a baby. These people were very much like modern man; there was a skull which showed a high forehead and a quite human chin.

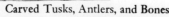
Carved Tusks, Antlers, and Bones

More remains of the Cro-Magnon type were found in other places, including England and Wales. In one place the bones of thousands of horses were found at the bottom of a steep cliff. Evidently hunters had rounded them up and driven them off the cliff — just as Indians in America used to hunt and kill buffaloes only a few hundred years ago.

Cro-Magnon Man

Furthermore, scientists discovered caves where the Cro-Magnon men had buried their dead, laying the bodies to rest with food and tools, as though for a journey.

Cro-Magnon man was certainly an ancestor of modern man — probably a very recent ancestor. What about Neanderthal? Might he have been an earlier ancestor? More and more new evidence pointed that way. In 1880 a heavy, Neanderthal-type jaw was found in Schipka, Czechoslovakia. In 1887 more Neanderthal skeletons were dug up in a cave called Spy in Belgium. These skeletons lay below bones of mammoths and rhinoceroses and stone axes and knives. There could be no doubt about the great age of these remains, for in this case the digging was done scientifically.

Virchow and the other skeptics were at last proved to be wrong. All these bones were not the remains of freakish modern men; Neanderthal was an early type, older and more primitive than Cro-Magnon man, but human for all that.

But what came before Neanderthal?

37

6

THE APE MAN OF JAVA

In Holland there was a young man named Eugene Dubois. He was born in 1858. As he grew up, he became fascinated by the mystery of Man's ancestors. He heard all the arguments about whether the Neanderthal men were the first human beings or not. Dubois thought not. He believed that the earliest men must have been more ape-like.

At any rate, he was sure that both Man and the apes had come from a common ancestor, from whom they had branched off as separate families.

Dubois studied medicine and became a teacher of anatomy. But all the time his secret thoughts were of that missing ancestor. What was he like? Where did he live? Dubois decided to look for him.

Where should he look? Not in Europe, for there were no apes there. He made up his mind that he would go to search on the islands of Java and Sumatra, where some of the great apes still lived.

In 1887 Dubois managed to get a job as a doctor in the Royal Dutch Army and he sailed for Sumatra.

Just as soon as he could, he began to spend his free hours hunting for fossils. He started searching in caves, but he soon realized that in that part of the world caves were not a likely place to find fossils. This was not like Europe, where large animals had lived in caves to escape the cold. In the tropical East Indies, about the only animals that lived in caves were bats and lizards. Besides, in that warm climate the remains of living things would decay very quickly.

Where, then, could Dubois expect to find fossils? Well, one possible place might be near volcanoes. Lava from the volcanoes might have buried animals and preserved them as it

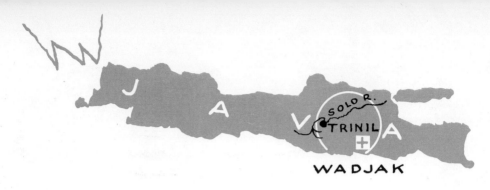

hardened into rock. And on the Island of Java there were some active volcanoes.

One day Dubois heard that a fossilized human skull had been found near Wadjak on the southern coast of Java. He managed to get the government to send him there. The fossils found near the coast, however, seemed too modern. So Dubois went inland to a place near the village of Trinil, on the Solo River, where the natives had seen many old bones which they thought were the bones of giants.

It was a peaceful spot. The slow-moving Solo River wound lazily through the fields. In the course of centuries, it had cut through layers of earth and rock, exposing the bones of many ancient animals.

Dubois began to dig. In November, 1890, he found a piece of a lower jaw, with one tooth.

The Solo River

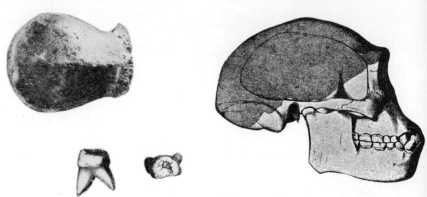
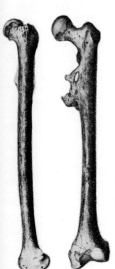

Skull-top, Leg Bones, and Teeth of Pithecanthropus

Then the rains began. Nobody could work in that steaming mud. Dubois had to stop. But the next year he came back and went on digging. He found another tooth.

In October, 1891, he found a dark brown bone sticking out of the rock. With as much care as if it had been a diamond, he dug it out. It was the top of a near-human skull. Dubois could hardly believe his luck. He had come halfway around the world and actually found the thing he had dreamed of finding!

The skull was low and flat and had a heavy ridge over the eyes and another at the back. It looked more like the skull of an ape than of a man. But it was too big for an ape!

Again the rains came, and Dubois went back to his job as Army doctor. But in 1892 he was back at Trinil. Layer by layer, he and his native helpers dug away the soil. Not far from the spot where the skull and the jawbone had turned up, he found a thigh bone. There was no doubt about it; the bone was human or very nearly human. Dubois' knowledge of anatomy told him that this was the leg bone of a creature who had stood and walked erect.

Did the skull and the leg bone belong to the same animal? He decided that they did. He named it *Pithecanthropus erectus* — the erect ape-man. He said it was the link between apes and men. In 1894 he published the story of his discovery. In 1895 he sailed back to Europe.

40

Was Dubois greeted with cheers and congratulations by the great scientists of Europe? He was not. When he exhibited the bones at the Congress of Anthropology, the famous Dr. Virchow pronounced the thigh bone human but declared that the skull was obviously that of an ape. The two bones therefore could not have belonged to the same individual. And he dismissed the jaw and teeth that Dubois had found as evidence too skimpy to prove anything.

Dubois fought for his theory about Pithecanthropus. He reasoned that the ape-man had been killed by a volcanic eruption and been washed down the river. Then crocodiles had eaten the body and scattered the bones about. But they had not scattered them far. All the bones had been found within a small area 46 yards long. And there were no other such bones for miles around. He pointed out that the teeth were both ape-like and human. He had measured the skull and found it midway in size between those of an ape and a man. He had made casts of the inside of the skull. These showed that the brain had been much like a human brain.

Some scientists agreed with Dubois. But others could not imagine that a creature so like an ape could have walked upright.

The arguments went on and on. Finally Dubois became so hurt and angry that he retired from the battle and went into seclusion. He packed up his bones, locked them in the museum of his home town, and for 30 years after that nobody got so much as a look at them.

Skull-caps of Ape, Pithecanthropus, and Modern Man

7

CLUES IN THE BONES

How in the world can the fossil hunters tell so much about an ancient animal by just looking at a bone? What made Eugene Dubois think that the piece of skull he had found belonged to an ape-man, and that the thigh bone showed that its owner walked erect? By what magic can anatomists, from just a remnant of a skeleton, draw a picture of a creature they have never seen?

Well, it is not really so mysterious as it seems. Remember that the shape of a bone must depend on the way it is used. Through evolution, an animal's body becomes adapted to its way of life. So the shape of a bone tells a lot about how its owner lived.

If you look at the skeletons of some animals that are alive today, such as those pictured here, you can see that these animals have a backbone. The backbone is very handy, because it provides a frame on which to hang legs and other organs, and it furnishes a bony housing to protect the soft, delicate spinal cord — the main trunk of the nervous system. Because the backbone is made up of sections named vertebrae, animals with backbones are called vertebrates.

The simplest vertebrate is the fish. Living in the water, it needs no legs; instead, it has fins for swimming. The fish reproduces by means of soft eggs which it lays in the water.

The lizard, a primitive land animal, has legs with which it waddles over the ground. It can live in the air because it has developed lungs for breathing. And its eggs, which it lays on the ground, are protected by a hard shell.

Primitive Vertebrates—a Fish and a Lizard

Skeletons of Dog, Ape, and Man

When we come to the warm-blooded mammals, such as the dog, we find that they are built much more efficiently for living in land environments. They have more energy, and for this they need to eat more. So they have bigger lungs, taking in more oxygen from the air to burn their food. See how much bigger the dog's ribs are than the lizard's. It also has more highly developed teeth and a better digestive system. Furthermore, the dog can run much faster than a lizard because its legs are set under its body, instead of out at the sides. And the toes on each foot, with claws on the ends, are useful for scratching and digging.

The dog's pelvis is larger, because a mammal does not lay eggs; the mother carries her babies inside her body until they are well developed. After a litter of puppies is born, the mother nurses them until they can take care of themselves. A baby lizard, on the other hand, is on its own as soon as it hatches out of its shell. It is born with instincts that help it to find food and hide from its enemies. But it does not develop further, except to

The Pelvic Bones of a Dog (*left*) and a Lizard (*right*)

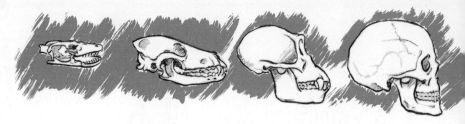

Skulls of Lizard, Dog, Chimpanzee, and Man

grow bigger. Because it has a very small brain, it cannot learn much.

Look at the dog's skull. Notice how much bigger its brain box is, compared to the size of its body, than the lizard's. Its brain is big enough to give it what we call intelligence. Of course, a dog, like the lower animals, also depends a great deal on instincts. But learning plays a much bigger part in its life.

Now look at the skeleton of the chimpanzee. It is far more highly developed than the dog's. The chimp has hands with separate thumbs that enable it to grasp things; it can swing on branches and live in trees. Its collarbones and shoulder blades allow it to reach out sideways with its arms and rotate them at the shoulder. And it has a big brain for its size.

Finally, compare the human skeleton with the chimp's. Whereas the chimp has bent legs and needs to touch its knuckles to the ground to keep its balance when it walks, a human being's leg and foot bones are so built that he can easily stand and walk erect. The feet point forward. The leg bones are long and straight, with ridges to which strong muscles are attached. The arms hang straight down from the shoulder and can rotate in all directions.

Skeletons of
Chimp and Man

Dog's Front Paw, Chimp's Foot, and Human Foot

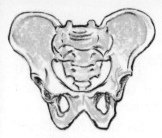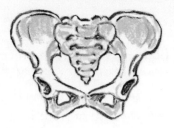

Pelvis of a Man (*left*), Woman (*middle*), and Female Chimp (*right*)

Notice especially the broad pelvis in the human skeleton. The pelvis of a human female is big so that the baby's head, which is huge compared to the rest of the body, can pass through when the baby is delivered at birth.

After this quick look at the anatomy of various animals, we can understand what kinds of clues a fossil detective watches out for. Suppose, for instance, that he found just the skulls of three creatures — a dog, a chimpanzee, and a man. How would he compare them?

In the first place, the dog's skull is distinguished by the fact that it has a long snout and practically no forehead. The ape's face does not jut out so far, and it does have a forehead rising above the face. Finally, the man's skull shows a rather small, flat face and a big, bulging forehead, holding a large forebrain.

The dog has a bony ridge along the top of its skull, to which the jaw muscles are attached. And the neck muscles are attached to another ridge at the back of the skull. These muscles must be very strong, for the dog, having no hands, must do everything with its teeth.

The ape has these ridges too, but they are smaller. Apes use their hands for grasping, but they use their jaws for fighting — that is, the males do. Female apes have smaller jaws and smaller skull ridges.

Modern man doesn't have these skull ridges at all.

Look at the position of the eyes. The dog's eyes are on the opposite sides of the head and separated by the ridge of the snout, so the two eyes may not see the same thing. But this doesn't matter much to the dog, for it depends more on its keen nose to tell it what is going on. In the ape and in man the eyes are in front. Both eyes look at an object together, from slightly different angles. This gives what we call stereoscopic vision, which allows us to judge depth and distance.

Notice that these important eyes are surrounded and protected by bone. In the ape there is a heavy ridge over them. In man, with his vertical forehead, this ridge has disappeared.

Now look at the bottom of each skull. It has a hole called the foramen magnum, through which the spinal cord passes

Eyes and Vision of Dog, Ape, and Man

down from the brain. In the dog, the foramen magnum is at the back of the skull, because the spinal column goes back horizontally, as it must in a four-legged animal. But in the ape this hole is farther forward under the skull, showing that the head is over the rest of the body and the animal has a more upright posture. In man, the foramen magnum is right in the middle of the bottom of the skull, because the head is balanced on top of the body and the spinal cord goes straight down.

This is one way to tell whether the animal walked upright or not.

We can learn a great deal, too, from the teeth. The fossil hunters find teeth more often than other bones, because they are

46

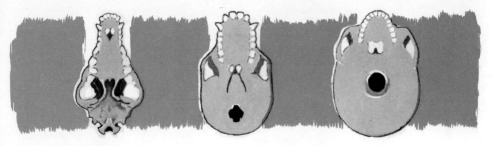

Foramen Magnum (*marked in black*) in Skulls of Dog, Ape, and Man

made of a harder material and are covered with strong enamel; the teeth are therefore more likely to be preserved for a long time.

The lower animals have either no teeth at all or only very simple ones. They usually swallow most of their food whole, and those that do have teeth use them merely to grab the food.

But a dog has teeth which are shaped for various purposes. Its front teeth are specialized for biting, and its back teeth for slicing and chewing meat, since a dog is a meat-eating creature. In a horse, the front teeth are large and protruding, for tearing up grass, and the back teeth are wide and flat, for grinding the grass. In squirrels, the front teeth are worn down by constant nibbling but keep on growing, so they do not wear out.

Now look at your own teeth. In front you have several incisors, which are upright and fairly sharp, for biting off bits of food. Next, on each side you have a canine tooth with one little point. Then come two bicuspids, each with two little

Teeth of Dog, Horse, and Squirrel

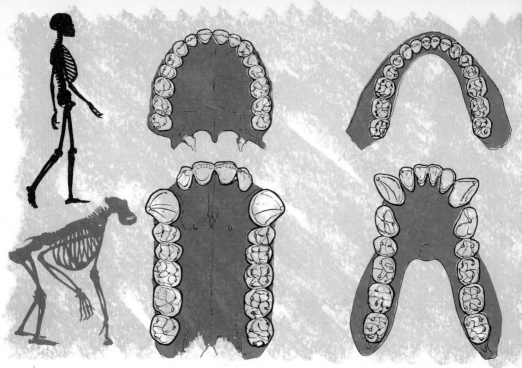

Teeth of Man (*top*) and Gorilla (*bottom*)

points or cusps. Then come three molars, with four or five cusps. These various back teeth are good for chewing many different kinds of food. They are all arranged in a rounded arch, and they are all pretty even in size.

As you know, human beings are "omnivorous" — they eat everything. Therefore it is very useful to have teeth which are not too special but can deal with all kinds of food.

An ape's teeth look quite different. One of the differences is a space in the upper jaw, just behind the front biting teeth, into which the lower canine tooth fits when the teeth are closed. The ape's back teeth are in a straight line rather than in an arch. This is what makes the jaw stick out as a kind of chinless snout.

As far as we know, all apes have this kind of tooth arrangement, while human beings do not. So, if you find a jawbone, or even some teeth, you can make a very good guess as to whether it belongs to an ape or a man or some form in between.

If you find even the top of a skull, you can tell what sort of animal it came from by the depth of the brain case and by the

48

ridges on it, or the lack of ridges. The size of the brain case is one of the best clues to distinguishing between an ape and a man. One good way to measure the brain capacity of a fossil skull is to fill the skull with something like sand or lead shot, then pour the amount it holds into a measuring jar.

The brain of modern man is between 1,200 and 1,500 cubic centimeters in size (one cubic centimeter is about one-eighth of a cubic inch). An ape's brain ranges from 300 to 650 c.c. So if you find a primate skull with a capacity somewhere between 600 and 1,200 c.c., it probably came from an ape-man.

Another way to judge the caliber of the brain that occupied the skull is to make a plaster cast of the inside of the skull. The folds and bumps on the brain leave their marks there, so a cast of the inside of the skull will show how well developed the brain was. If you find that the part of the brain that controls speech was well developed, that is pretty good evidence that the ape-man knew how to talk.

In this way, from pieces of head bone, scientists are often able to reconstruct the whole skull and even model a face to go over it.

Leg bones likewise tell about the creature's habits and movements. For instance, the grooves and ridges on a leg bone, showing where the muscles were attached, tell how the animal walked. And the size of the leg bones gives an idea of how big the creature was.

That is the way fossil hunters are able to give a description of the creature whose bones they have found, to give the creature a name, and to put together pieces of the puzzle about our ancestors. It was this kind of evidence that made Dubois sure that Pithecanthropus was an ape-man. And eventually the doubters had to admit that he was right.

8

MAN OF CHINA

Scientists did not forget Pithecanthropus after he was put away. And as more new fossils were discovered, they became eager to have another look at him.

This wish rose to a high pitch in 1920 when a fossil skull was found in Australia. Australia, once connected to Antarctica and South Africa, has been a separate continent for 70 million years. Finding a human fossil there was strange and surprising. It might mean that Australia was the birthplace of the human race! So the fossil hunters wanted very much to compare the Australian skull with Pithecanthropus.

At last, in 1923, Dubois came out of seclusion. He said that he was ready to show his fossils. Not only that. He had a big surprise. He had two other skulls from Java that nobody else had ever seen. He hadn't mentioned them because he wanted all the attention given to Pithecanthropus. Both of these other skulls, from Wadjak, were bigger than the one from Trinil. They were even bigger than the average European skull.

Scientists now came to Leyden in Holland to see and touch these bits of bone, about which there had been so much commotion. This time they were more impressed by Pithecanthropus. He certainly seemed to be a creature between ape and man. The shape of his brain, which could be told by the shape of the inside of his skull, looked human. The part of the brain that controlled speech seemed to be well developed. And if he really could walk upright, he must have been somewhere on the way to being a man. But more evidence was needed.

50

The evidence came a few years later. And it came from two directions at once. The first clue was from a place far away from Java — a hill near Peking, China.

A German doctor traveling in China had found an old Chinese medical book and translated it with the help of a friend who knew the language well. He discovered that the book had some amazing ideas about the powers of "dragon bones." According to the authors of the book, these bones, when ground up and boiled or fried, would cure practically anything that ailed the human system — a stomach ache, nightmares, boils, even shyness!

The doctor learned that the "dragon bones" were actually fossils. Every year *tons* of fossil bones were being dug out of caves in the mountains and sold in drugstores. If you went to a Chinese drugstore with the right prescription, you could buy teeth and bones of all kinds. And this had been going on for centuries.

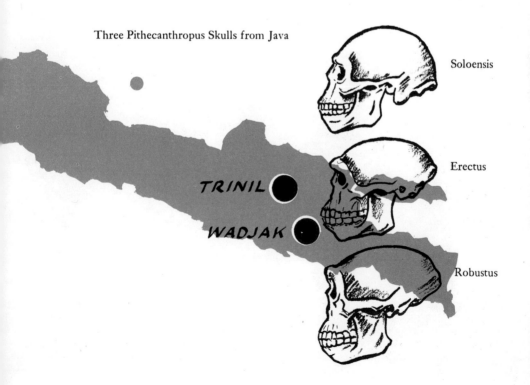

Three Pithecanthropus Skulls from Java

Soloensis

Erectus

TRINIL

WADJAK

Robustus

The doctor was tremendously excited. He spent all his money for "dragon bones" and took them back to Germany to study. When he studied them, he found he had a treasure beyond anything he had imagined. There were bones of extinct reptiles and mammals that nobody had even seen.

After he announced his news, expeditions of European scientists set out at once to hunt for fossils in the rich hills of China. They unearthed dinosaur bones and eggs and huge extinct mammals millions of years old.

Of all the bones the doctor had brought back from Chinese drugstores, the most interesting was a single tooth. It looked human! Where had it been found? Of course the druggists could not tell him.

But the question was followed up by a Swedish geologist named Andersson, who was working for the Chinese government as an adviser. He learned that many fossils had been found at a place near Peking called Chicken-Bone Hill. Andersson got permission to go and dig there.

Fossil Eggs of Protoceratops, a Dinosaur of Ancient China

But permission from the government wasn't quite enough. The village people weren't willing at all. They thought it was bad luck for foreigners to come and dig up the bones of creatures which had been dead so long. They sat down in the diggers' excavations and yelled at them to go away.

One of Andersson's Chinese friends said the digging was good at another place called Dragon-Bone Hill, near the village of Chou-kou-tien. So Andersson decided to go there. At Dragon-Bone Hill he found no human bones, but something just as interesting. He found pieces of quartz.

Now quartz did not belong in that hill. This kind of rock came from far away. The pieces of quartz must have been brought there, to be used for some purpose. And only one creature would do that.

Andersson said: "Primitive man lived here. All we need to do is dig for him."

So the excavation proceeded. By 1926 the bones of about 20 different mammals had been found — bears, hyenas, horses, and many others. And best of all, two almost human teeth appeared. Primitive man might indeed have lived there.

Protoceratops

Fossil "dragon" teeth.

The three at the top belonged to a giant man.

The news was interesting to scientists everywhere, but most of all to Davidson Black, a professor at Peking Medical College. Dr. Black, who had come from Canada, was fascinated with human anatomy, paleontology, and adventure. He had an idea that Man had originated in Asia. That was why he was working in Peking. In his spare time he went fossil hunting.

Andersson took the two teeth from Dragon-Bone Hill to Dr. Black. Dr. Black was so excited that he got an American foundation to give him money for a scientific expedition.

Dr. Black

In April, 1927, the expedition went to work in the valley near Chou-kou-tien. They tackled some limestone caves which were thousands of years old and filled up with rock and all kinds of rubbish.

The digging was very hard work. The rock had to be blasted away, and then every crumb of rock had to be examined for clues. Imagine looking for bits of bone in a mountain of broken rock!

To make things just a little harder, war had broken out in China. Soldiers often interrupted the diggers' work. But in spite of everything, they succeeded in finding hundreds of animal fossils.

Yet they were disappointed. October 19, the day they would have to stop work, was approaching and they had not found any sign of man. Then, on the 16th of October, luck smiled on them. They found a human tooth. Just one tooth, stuck in the rock, near the spot where Andersson had found the first two teeth.

Dr. Black compared it with hundreds of other teeth, ancient and modern. It was human, all right. It was a lower molar, very large and wrinkled. The tooth was different enough from other human teeth so that Dr. Black was sure it belonged to a separate race of men. He gave it a name: *Sinanthropus Pekinensis* (Chinese Man of Peking).

54

The digging went on. In 1928 two jaws, some skull bones, and about 20 teeth were found. And then came the greatest thrill of all.

At the end of November, 1929, one of the workers opened a deep cave. This young man was a Chinese named Weng Chung Pei. He had been well trained as a paleontologist. The remarkable thing about him was that he never became discouraged, even when everybody else was about ready to give up. The weather was very cold, and the expedition was about to stop work. But Weng had himself let down on a rope into the cave. There was nothing there, so he went into the next cave. He poked about in some rubbish on the floor. There, right at his feet, he found a fossilized skull — a whole human skull!

Could anything have been more exciting?

The next day the block of stone holding the skull was cut out and wrapped in paper and cloth. It was sent off to Black in his Peking laboratory.

When he saw the skull, Dr. Black was the happiest man in the world. He called in all his friends and gave a party to welcome a man half a million years old.

Hard work was still ahead. It took a long time to chip away the stone around the fossil. But when the skull was

Dragon Bone Hill. The digging areas are divided into sections.

Weng being lowered into cave, and (*at right, below*) the skull he found.

finally freed of the rock, Black and his co-workers could see an amazing resemblance to the skull of Pithecanthropus.

The Chinese skull, however, was much more complete than the Java skull, and it was clear that it belonged to a man, not an ape. This was the evidence that was needed. If Sinanthropus was human, then Pithecanthropus, whose skullcap was so similar, must be human too.

The men went back to work with renewed vigor. But enthusiasm was not enough. This work took money, too. Dr. Black managed to persuade the Rockefeller Foundation to provide money. A research laboratory was set up, as a department of the Chinese Geological Survey.

In 1930 Weng Chung Pei dug out another skull from the same cave. This one was not all in one piece, but the workers fitted the fragments together with great care.

Dr. Black studied all the specimens and wrote descriptions of them. He worked very hard, usually at night, when he would not be disturbed. It was too much for his bad heart, which he kept a secret from his friends so that no one would try to stop him from finishing his work on Peking man. One day in 1934 his secretary found him dead of a heart attack at his desk, with the skull of Sinanthropus in his hands.

At first it seemed that the work could not go on without him. But the following year the Rockefeller Foundation sent a scientist to carry on. He was Franz Weidenreich, an anthropologist who had made many studies comparing the skeletons of apes and Man.

Dr. Weidenreich believed that the first step in the evolution from ape to Man was the change to walking upright. Therefore the most important clue was the shape of the leg and pelvis. After that, the main clues for deciding whether a fossil was human were the shape of the teeth and the size of the skull.

All the evidence of Sinanthropus' skull proved that he was human. But in addition, the caves near Chou-kou-tien showed something more. Buried in the rocks were thousands of chipped stone tools and pieces of bone that looked as if they had been used as tools. There were bits of charred bone and charcoal, which showed that Peking man had known how to use fire. There were piles of bones from animals that he must have killed — deer, sheep, bison, mammoths, camels, wild boars, and others. Many of the long bones had been split open,

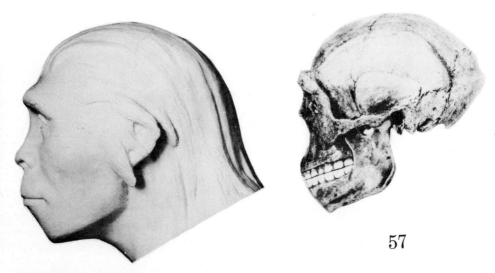

57

Skull of Sinanthropus woman. At the left is a reconstruction of her head made by Franz Weidenreich and Lucile Swan.

probably so that he could eat the marrow. There were seed shells from small fruits.

Now it was 1941, and war was coming closer. Dr. Weidenreich was in the United States. The director of the Chinese Geological Survey thought that the collection of fossils should be sent to the United States for safety. The bones were packed in glass jars and put into a trunk to be taken home by a detachment of Marines.

On December 5 they were put on a train. On December 7 war broke out. The train was captured by Japanese. Nobody knows, to this day, what happened to the fossils. Some say they were put on a boat which was later sunk. Some say that the soldiers who captured the train either threw the fossils away, thinking them worthless, or sold them for dragon bones.

Casts had been made of some of the bones. These are in the American Museum of Natural History. We also have the notes on studies of the bones made in the laboratory. But the bones themselves are gone.

MEANWHILE, BACK IN JAVA

9

While all the exploration was going on near Chou-kou-tien, things were happing in other parts of the world too.

In 1930 G. H. R. von Koenigswald, a young German paleontologist working in a Munich museum, was asked by one of his former professors whether he would like to go to Java to work for the Dutch Geological Survey. More information was wanted about Pithecanthropus. The young man was delighted to go.

He arrived in Java in 1931. With his helpers he set out at once for Trinil, where Dubois had made his discoveries so many years before. They had to start early in the morning to avoid the hot mid-day sun. On the way they passed volcanoes, live ones that belched lava and ashes, and dead ones that belched no more. They saw hills covered with teak forests, fields of rice and sugar cane, coconut palms, and villages full of people. Java has more people per square mile than almost any other spot on earth. They passed men and women going

von Koenigswald

to market, barefoot, with straw hats on their heads to keep off the sun. They saw water buffaloes with little boys riding on their backs.

At last they came to the village of Trinil. There was the Solo River — broad, brown, and muddy. Buffaloes and people bathed in it; clothes and teeth were washed in it. People drank the water and cooked with it, knowing nothing about germs.

Now women and children began to run after the scientists with black stones to sell. These were fossils. They were bones and teeth and pieces of antlers. Some of the teeth were huge. They came from enormous extinct pigs and rhinoceroses and from an ancestor of the elephant called the stegodon.

At a place on the river banks, von Koenigswald saw a stone with an inscription saying that *Pithecanthropus erectus* had been found 192 yards east-northeast of the spot.

The work of the new expedition was to find out the ages of the various layers of earth and rock. They hoped to do this by recognizing the fossils buried in each layer. At different times in the past there had been land bridges between Java and the mainland of Asia. Ice Age animals could easily have walked across. By their remains, the scientists could identify the strata in Java, where there had been no Ice Age.

Stegodon, Pig, and Rhinoceros of Ancient Java

The expedition got busy digging out and classifying fossils around Trinil. Many of the bones proved to be from the same kinds of animals that paleontologists had found in the Chinese drug stores.

Buffalo Skull

However, the Trinil diggings didn't give the expedition the information it wanted. There was only one layer of deposits. So there was no way of telling which creatures arrived first.

One day a member of the expedition named Ter Har discovered a new site. He had been making a geological map of the area around Ngandong, a village some distance from Trinil. While resting by the riverside, suddenly he noticed, high above the river bed, a layer of sand and gravel which the river must have deposited very long ago, when it was much higher. He poked around in the bank and found a large buffalo skull.

The next day the expedition went to work on this layer. The diggers soon found a treasure of fossils. There were bones of all kinds of animals, lying in three different strata.

The workers wrapped the bones carefully in paper and sent them to the laboratory at Bandung. To the paleontologists' great surprise, some human skulls turned up in the collection. What was especially surprising was that these were younger than Pithecanthropus; in fact, they were Neanderthal skulls!

After Fuhlrott's discovery of the first Neanderthal remains in Germany, other Neanderthal men had been found elsewhere in Europe and even in Africa. Now here was a Neanderthal type far away in Asia! Neanderthal and his cousins must have roamed over most of the ancient world.

This latest find was named Solo man, after the River Solo. More skulls of the same type turned up in the diggings at Ngandong. Some leg bones were found, too.

One interesting thing about these Solo skulls was that in all but two the bottom of the skull was smashed. This probably means that the skulls were trophies of ancient head hunters.

61

Skulls of Neanderthal *(left)* and Pithecanthropus

Even today there are some head-hunting tribes whose warriors smash the skulls of their enemies and eat the brains. Some of these peoples believe that by eating the brains they will absorb the wisdom and strength of their victims. It is really a compliment to the defeated enemy.

Who was Solo man? Was he an ancestor of the living Australian natives whose skulls resemble his, and whom white men found when they discovered that continent? Or did he belong to the same period as the Neanderthals of Europe, who lived from about 100,000 to 40,000 years ago? In recent years anthropologists have been more and more interested in the mystery of where Neanderthal fits in among our ancestors.

But let's get back to von Koenigswald's search for more remains of Pithecanthropus. He was still looking for clues to the age of that ape-man.

At Modjokerto in Java, in deposits that seemed older than those at Trinil, diggers found the skull of a human child. In the same stratum were remains of types of animals that go back nearly a million years. One of them, for instance, was the Leptobos, a primitive ox which is found in the beginning of the first Ice Age in Europe and in India.

This might be a clue to the age of Pithecanthropus. If the Modjokerto deposits were older than those at Trinil, then the skull that Dubois found at Trinil must date from the Middle Pleistocene. That would mean, von Koenigswald thought, that Pithecanthropus lived about 400,000 or 500,000 years ago.

The Modjokerto skull looked like a baby Pithecanthropus. But Dubois, now an old man, said that was impossible. He had changed his mind; Pithecanthropus, which he had originally called an ape-man, was not human after all, he said. Since the child's skull was clearly human, it could not be Pithecanthropus.

Von Koenigswald did not agree. He went hunting for more evidence. In 1934 he started digging at a promising new site in East Java at a village named Sangiran.

It was the dry season, and the air was clear. There were great volcanoes all about, and on the hills were blocks of volcanic rock that had once been molten lava. The landscape had a weird look.

The natives were very helpful. They showed the scientists where the best beds of fossils lay. There were bones of saber-toothed tigers, hyenas, and tapirs. Von Koenigswald felt sure that if he could only stay long enough, he would find human fossils.

But he was running out of money. Soon he would have no money to pay his helpers. What should he do? He simply could not stop now.

A friend wrote to the Carnegie Institution in Washington. As a result, von Koenigswald was invited to Philadelphia to attend a congress on fossil man. There he was given a grant of money to go on with his work.

He quickly wrote to his faithful assistant Atma, in Java, telling him to start digging again. He himself started back to Java, by way of China. In China, he visited Chou-kou-tien and talked with Dr. Weidenreich. He also went on a tour of Chinese drugstores, looking for dragons' teeth.

No sooner was he back in Java than he got some good news. A piece of a jaw which was definitely human had been found at Sangiran. Near it was a piece of skull.

Von Koenigswald started a vigorous search for the rest of the skull. He offered his native helpers ten cents for every piece of skull they found. This was an unheard-of price for fossils, and it soon got results. The same day little pieces of bone began to arrive — lots of them. The natives were playing a clever trick on von Koenigswald. In order to get more money, they were breaking up the skull sections they found into small pieces! But fortunately the damage could be fixed. Von Koenigswald was able to fit the pieces together. By the end of the day he had all the pieces and rebuilt a practically complete skull.

This was a great day. It ended with a feast, with music and dancing.

The skull was exactly like the original Pithecanthropus, only more complete. Von Koenigswald immediately sent a photograph and a letter to Dubois, thinking Dubois would be just as pleased as he was. But no! Dubois crankily denied that it was the real thing. He said the picture had been faked. Besides, he insisted that Pithecanthropus was an ape.

But everyone else agreed that it was a wonderful find. This and the original Trinil skull were as much alike as two peas.

Now to compare it with Peking man. Von Koenigswald went to Peking. He and Dr. Weidenreich laid their specimens out on a table. Pithecanthropus and Sinanthropus lay side by side. And they turned out to be alike in nearly every way!

Dr. Black had predicted that the two types would be

found to be related. He was right, as the proof now showed.

Now another mystery arose. Von Koenigswald's workers had found a piece of an upper jaw which looked very peculiar. The teeth were human, but very large. Furthermore, between the canine and the last incisor was a space known as the "simian gap." This space appears in the jaws of apes but is never found in a human jaw.

Von Koenigswald's workers found the rest of the skull. When he put all the pieces together, he saw that it was like the Pithecanthropus skulls, but thicker and heavier.

Why was it different from the others? Weidenreich thought that this might be the skull of a male Pithecanthropus and the others of females. But von Koenigswald found that the new skull had been dug up from a deeper level than the Pithecanthropus bones found earlier. In fact, it seemed to

Dr. Weidenreich and Dr. von Koenigswald examine a giant skull from Java.

belong to the same age as the baby Pithecanthropus found in the old deposits at Modjokerto. So it probably was an early type of Pithecanthropus.

The very large teeth were especially interesting to von Koenigswald. In his prowling among Chinese drugstores, he had found three human-looking molar teeth which were simply enormous. They were so big that Weidenreich insisted they must come from an ape. He called the creature Gigantopithecus.

In Java some more very large teeth were found. It didn't seem possible that a human jaw could hold them. Then, in 1941, a workman sent in a piece of a lower jaw which was as big as a gorilla's jaw but had three teeth which looked very human. Also, inside the jaw there was a little bump, which to a scientist was an important clue: it was the bump to which are attached tongue muscles used for talking! No ape could have had this bump. The jaw must be human.

It looked as if its owner must have been a giant. If the rest of his body was in proportion, he must have been eight feet tall. Of course, it was possible that he was not so huge but just had an unusually big jaw.

Jaws of Modern Man *(left)*, Meganthropus *(center)*, and Gorilla *(right)*

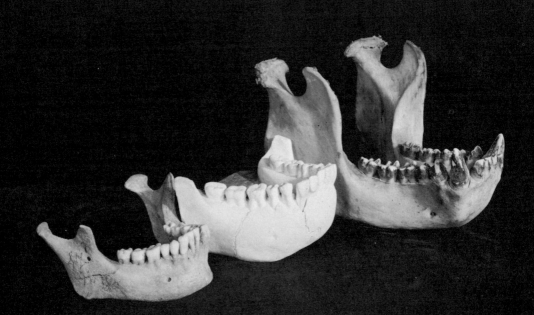

Anyway, von Koenigswald called the big-jawed man *Meganthropus Palaeojavanicis*—Giant Man of Ancient Java.

One thing was clear. There must have been several types of primitive men, both in China and in Java.

The Japanese were invading Southeast Asia. Von Koenigswald knew he might be caught in the war. Whatever happened, he wanted his precious collection to be safe. So he sent plaster casts of his fossils to Dr. Weidenreich, who had gone to New York.

Then the Japanese occupied Java. All through World War II, there was no further word from von Koenigswald. Nobody even knew whether he was alive or not. But he was, very much so.

Afraid that the Japanese might destroy his fossils, von Koenigswald hid them and showed the Japanese only plaster casts, carefully colored so that they would look like the fossils themselves. He hid the originals in the houses of friends. He put one collection of teeth in a big milk bottle and buried it.

At the end of the war von Koenigswald was finally released from the Japanese prison camp. All his fossils were saved. One skull had been given to the Japanese emperor as a birthday present, but even this was returned.

Von Koenigswald went to New York to work with Weidenreich. There for the first time he learned the sad fate of the Peking man fossils — that all of them had been taken by Japanese soldiers and had disappeared.

How lucky it was that Weidenreich still had plaster copies! Every piece in the puzzle of early man was becoming more and more important. For by this time anthropologists were beginning to feel that they were coming closer to solving some of the mysteries. Exciting new discoveries were turning up in Africa. Pieces of the puzzle were fitting into place.

But there were some peculiar pieces that still confused everybody. The most peculiar was the case of Piltdown man.

THE FORGED FOSSIL 10

In 1908 a gentleman named Charles Dawson, who was an amateur archaeologist and liked to collect fossils, was taking a walk near the village of Piltdown, not far from London. He saw some men working in a gravel pit. He thought it looked like a good place to find fossils, and he asked the workmen, if they saw something interesting, to save it for him.

A few days later one of the men did find a piece of bone. It was part of a skull, and it was very thick. The bone was reddish brown, like the stones in the gravel pit.

Dawson began to dig in the pit himself. He searched for a long time, and finally he found some more pieces. Then he asked a famous British paleontologist, Sir Arthur Smith-Woodward, to come and help him. In the spring of 1912 they found another piece of the skull. Later a very large canine tooth, badly worn, also turned up.

When Smith-Woodward put all the pieces together, they formed an amazing creature. The brain case was clearly human. But the jaw was exactly like an ape's! Here was a man with an ape's jaw!

There were other puzzles, too. In the same pit, Dawson and Smith-Woodward found some rough stone tools and teeth and bones of elephants, hippopotamuses, and other animals, including an extinct beaver. Some of these animals had lived at one time, some at another. To which of these periods did the Piltdown man belong? Had he lived at the time of the elephant or the later time of the beaver? And did the stone tools belong to him?

The Piltdown fossil came to be called *Eoanthropus dawsoni,* or "the Dawn Man." There were endless learned discussions about him. Some authorities said he came from the early Pleistocene, some said even earlier. Some thought the Dawn Man was really a woman. Trying to explain the combination of a human brain with an ape-like jaw, some said that Man might not have developed a human jaw until after his brain developed.

A few anthropologists insisted that the brain case and the jaw could not belong to the same creature. But they were in a minority. All the books written about human evolution listed Piltdown man as an early human specimen. And for more than 30 years the fossil lay in the museum, causing a great deal of trouble to anthropologists and mystifying everybody.

Then in 1948 scientific detectives solved the mystery.

A young English geologist and anthropologist named Kenneth Oakley had become interested in a chemical method of dating old bones. This method involved the element fluorine. As you probably know, dentists have discovered that fluorine has important effects on teeth. People who live in places where there is a small amount of fluorine compounds (fluorides) in the drinking water have few or no cavities in their teeth. Now it has also been known for some time that bones in the soil absorb some fluoride. The longer they have been buried, the more fluoride the bones contain.

So Oakley worked out a method of telling the age of buried bones and fossils by measuring the amount of fluoride in them. He tried this test on a number of old animal bones and human fossils. His test worked. Bones of the same known age had a certain percentage of fluoride, and the percentage depended on the age: it was higher in older bones, lower in more recent ones.

Dr. Oakley

Dr. Oakley and his helpers then tested the Piltdown fossils. Using a dentist's drill, they took small samples from the Pilt-down man's skull and from the animals found with him. The elephant and hippopotamus bones turned out to have quite a bit of fluoride and clearly were very old. But the skull had only a small amount — about one-fifth of 1 per cent! It could not be nearly as ancient as had been thought. As a matter of fact, the skull turned out to be only about 20,000 years old!

No wonder the brain case looked so human. It belonged to a modern man. What about the jaw, then? According to the fluoride test, the jaw also was recent. But it certainly could not go with the brain case of a modern man.

To find out whether the jaw and the brain case were of the same age, Dr. Oakley applied another test. This one is based on the amount of nitrogen in the bones. After a living creature dies, the bones begin to lose nitrogen. So the older they are, the less nitrogen they have. Dr. Oakley measured the nitrogen in the jaw and in the skull. He found that the jaw had much less than the skull did. The skull and the jaw did not belong together after all. The owner of the skull had died long before the owner of the jaw!

Oakley and his fellow detectives now suspected that someone had played a trick. They looked at the tooth under a microscope and discovered that it had been filed down to make it look worn. They also found that the bones had been stained with a brown dye to make to make them look very old.

Finally, it turned out that the reason the jaw looked so much like an ape's jaw was that it actually *was* an ape's jaw! Anatomists identified it as the jaw of an orangutan.

So the whole thing was nothing but a fraud. But such a clever fraud! Who could have perpetrated it? Was it Charles Dawson? Had he planted the forged fossils as a joke on the scientists? Or did someone else do it to fool *him?* Dawson died in 1916, so it was too late to ask him questions.

Probably we shall never know who forged the "Piltdown man." But at least the detectives got rid of a false clue. Anthropologists were relieved. Their faith in their picture of early man's anatomy was restored. The link between Man and the apes was not half man and half ape but something in between.

By this time the search for the missing link was getting warmer. The scene of the story now shifts to Africa, where some surprising new fossils had turned up.

Dr. Dart

11

MAN-APES IN AFRICA

Darwin suggested that Man might have originated in Africa, the home of gorillas and chimpanzees. The trouble is that the forests and jungles of tropical Africa, though they make a fine home for live apes, are a very poor place to find fossils. In that kind of place, even the bones of animals decay and disappear soon after they die.

It is true that in 1914 some farmers found the top of a large skull that might be human at Boskop in the Transvaal, and in 1922 others found in Rhodesia a clearly human skull of a creature with heavy brow ridges and a jutting jaw. But the Boskop skull cap did not tell much, and the Rhodesian skull turned out to be just another type of Neanderthal.

The big discovery came not in central Africa but in South Africa. The southern part of Africa happens to be a good place for preserving fossils. It is high, dry, and cool. During the last million years and more it has not been disturbed by glaciers, earthquakes, or mountain-building. However, the fossil hunters had not thought of looking for early man there, because apes do not live in a dry, cool climate.

But in 1923 a lucky find suddenly changed the whole picture.

Dr. Raymond Dart, an Englishman who was keenly interested in fossils, was on his way to South Africa to take a job as professor of anatomy at the University of Johannesburg. On the ship he met a nurse who told him that one of her patients, a diamond miner, had found a strange skull. It was too big to belong to a baboon, a kind of monkey that was known to live in that region.

Dr. Dart was so intrigued that after arriving in South Africa he tried to find the miner. He didn't succeed, but good fortune came to him from another direction. One day a student brought him a fossil skull in a piece of rock that had been blasted out of limestone in a mine at a place called Taungs. There was nothing unusual about the skull itself: it was just the skull of a baboon. But in the top of the skull was a hole that looked as if someone had bashed the baboon over the head with a club!

What ancient creature had done that? Was it possible that the baboon had been killed by some club-wielding early man?

Professor Dart went to see the manager of the mine at Taungs. Yes, the skull had been found in his mine. As a matter of fact, said the manager, his miners often dug up fossils.

The professor eagerly asked the manager to send him any fossils they might come across.

Baboon and Prehistoric Hunter

A week later, a box arrived. When it was delivered, Dr. Dart happened to be dressing for a wedding at which he was to be the best man. But he was so impatient to see what was in the box that he stopped to open it.

The professor almost didn't get to the wedding. The first thing he saw, right on top of the opened box, was a stone cast of the inside of a skull. The skull itself had broken away. Dart tore off his necktie and began digging into the box to see if the skull was there. It was, embedded in a block of stone!

At this point his wife showed up and pulled him away. The wedding guests were already arriving. He would simply have to put aside his precious skull until after the wedding.

As soon as the wedding was over, Dart rushed back to his room. First he carefully examined the cast of the inside of the skull. The brain was too small for a man. It must have belonged to an ape.

But this was a funny place to find an ape. South Africa is a land of grassy plains, and has been for at least a million years. Apes like trees and usually live on forest fruits. Here an ape would have had to move about on the ground and live, like the baboons and other monkeys, on a varied diet of whatever it could pick up — insects, lizards, birds' eggs, berries, grubs, and so on. If the fossil was indeed an ape, it must have been a very special kind of ape.

Dart lost no time in attacking the block of stone that held the skull. He chipped away at it with his wife's steel knitting needles. It was slow, delicate work, and he spent all his spare time working at the job of picking the stone away from the skull. It took him more than two months. At last, on Christmas Day in 1924, the skull was finally free. And what a Christmas present it turned out to be!

The whole face of the skull was in one piece, and Dart got a good view of how the creature must have looked. It had small, even, human-looking teeth and a vertical forehead, instead of the sloping forehead of Neanderthal. There were no big ridges over the eyes.

As Dart held the little skull in his hand, he felt sure that this creature must have walked upright and looked straight forward at the world.

What was especially appealing about the skull was that it had belonged to a very young child. For this reason the fossil came to be known as "Dart's baby."

What was it, really? Was it an ape or a human being? Dart had to decide what to call it. He quickly came to the conclusion that it could not be human — its brain was definitely too small. So Dart named the creature Australopithecus ("Southern Ape").

He reported his find to the world in an article in the British scientific magazine *Nature*. In this article he said that Australopithecus seemed to be a link between the apes and Man.

Like most announcements of new finds, Dart's article immediately started a big debate. Many scientists believed that he had gone too far and should have studied the skull longer before making such a positive statement about it. They said it looked somewhat human only because it was a baby's skull; an adult Australopithecus, they insisted, probably would not look human at all. Some made fun of "Dart's baby."

One man who took it seriously was a Scottish doctor named Robert Broom. Like Dart, Dr. Broom was a great hunter of fossils in his spare time. In fact, he was in Africa on a vacation studying fossils of early mammals when Dart announced the discovery of Australopithecus. Dr. Broom rushed to Johannesburg. After examining the skull, he decided that Dart was right. If this was not the missing link, it was something very close to it.

The rest of the world soon forgot the Taungs baby. But not Dart and Broom. They studied the skull very carefully,

The Taungs Baby

Antelope

Turtle

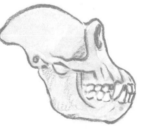

Ape

especially the teeth, and they were convinced it was a close relative of Man.

They found more reason for thinking so when they explored some caves near the Taungs mine. In these caves they discovered collections of bones of animals — antelopes, baboons, lizards, turtles, and so forth. The baboons all had

Lizards

their skulls bashed in, apparently by some kind of weapon. The collections of bones in the caves and the broken skulls spoke in favor of the idea that the animals were killed for food by a tool-using creature.

Another interesting fact was that the killed animals were almost always *young*. Perhaps they were the only ones the man-apes could catch. A full-grown antelope, for instance, would be too swift for an ape to catch, but by waiting at a water hole the hunter might be able to pounce and capture a baby antelope.

Dr. Dart could not continue his explorations any longer. He had to go back to his teaching job at the University. Dr. Broom also would have had to return to practicing medicine to make a living, but he had better luck. General Jan Smuts, the prime minister of South Africa at the time, decided to help him stay on to track down the mystery of Man's ancestors. Smuts got Dr. Broom an appointment as curator of paleontology and anthropology at the Transvaal Museum.

So, at the age of 68, Dr. Broom was at last able to spend all his time at the work he loved best. He got busy at once.

He went tramping through mines and quarries in South Africa. The doctor became a well-known figure in these places. Wherever he went, he was always neatly dressed in a dark suit and fresh white shirt. While his helpers, in shorts and sport shirts, sweated in the hot sun, Dr. Broom looked as if he had just stepped out of an air-conditioned room.

Near Johannesburg, at a place called Sterkfontein, was a limestone cave — one of the few in South Africa. Some baboon skulls had been found in the cave. The manager, a Mr. Barlow, had seized the opportunity to start a sightseeing business. He put out a guidebook saying: "Come to Sterkfontein and find the missing link."

Dr. Broom of course went to see Mr. Barlow. He asked the manager to be on the lookout for fossils of man-apes like the Taungs baby.

Eleven days later, Barlow had something for him. He handed Dr. Broom a stone brain cast.

"Is this what you want?" he asked.

It certainly was. The cast apparently came from an adult man-ape! Broom and his assistants dug into the rock where the cast had been found, and they soon picked up most of the skull.

There was no doubt that the skull belonged to a man-ape of a type like the one at Taungs. Broom named it *Plesianthropus transvaalensis* — "near-man of the Transvaal."

More excitement was in store for Dr. Broom.

One day in June of 1938 he visited Sterkfontein and was greeted by Barlow with the words:

"I have something nice for you today."

It was a piece of an upper jaw, with one tooth in place. This bone looked different from those of the Taungs and Plesianthropus fossils.

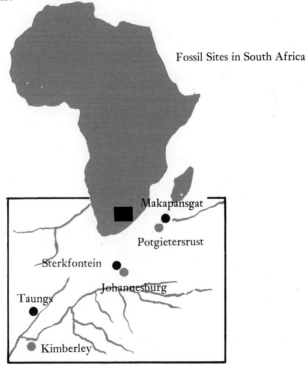

Fossil Sites in South Africa

Makapansgat

Potgietersrust

Sterkfontein

Johannesburg

Taungs

Kimberley

Broom, trying to hold in his excitement so that Barlow would not ask a high price for the jaw, said casually:

"It's pretty good. I'll give you a quid for it. Where did you find it?"

Barlow wouldn't tell. Broom finally had to appeal to him for the sake of his country and of science to reveal the place where the rest of the skull might be found.

Barlow then admitted that he had not found the fossil himself. It had been brought to him by a schoolboy named Gert Terblanche. The boy had picked it up on a nearby farm called Kromdraai.

Broom hurried to the boy's house. Gert was away in school, but his sister was at home. She took Broom to the field where her brother had found the bone, sticking out of a rock.

Broom looked around and found some more pieces of bone and two teeth. When he picked up the teeth, the girl said:

"Oh, my brother has more teeth like that in his pocket."

Broom rushed off to the school. The principal called Gert from class. The boy was pretty surprised to see his gray-haired visitor, but he readily handed over the teeth.

The scientist turned to the principal and asked:

"May I tell the children about these fossils and why they are important?"

The entire student body came to the assembly hall. For an hour and a half Dr. Broom talked to them about early man and his ancestors, while the students listened spellbound.

Then Broom and Gert hurried back to the farm. The boy brought out the lower jaw, which he had hidden away. Out to the field they went to look for more pieces of the skull. By the time they were through, they had found most of the left side of the skull and also some leg bones.

After putting the skull together, Broom saw that it was different in a number of ways from the Taungs baby and

78

Taungs Baby

Plesianthropus

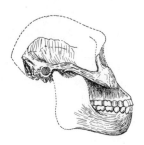

Paranthropus

Plesianthropus. The teeth were more human in shape; the face was flatter; the jaw and teeth were bigger. So here was a third type of man-ape. Broom named it *Paranthropus robustus* — "robust near-man."

Obviously the three types had lived at different periods; maybe they were related. Some of the animals found with the skulls at Sterkfontein and at Taungs were very old; animals like them in Europe were known to go back a million or two million years. On the other hand, at the Kromdraai site there were bones of types of horses that lived perhaps 800,000 years ago. So the three man-apes might span a long time and three different periods.

But one thing was sure. All three had walked erect like men. This was especially clear from the Kromdraai bones. The opening at the bottom of the skull, where the head connected with the spine, was far forward, showing that the creature held his head erect. The leg bones showed that he stood upright. From the size of the leg bones, it was possible to tell that Paranthropus was a little less than five feet tall — about the height of the present-day primitive Bushmen of South Africa.

Prehistoric Horses

In 1946 Broom summed up the story of the finds in Africa in a book called *The South African Fossil Ape Men.* Even the scientists who had had doubts were now convinced that these discoveries were really important. They began to follow the news from South Africa with growing excitement.

The main question is: How close were these man-apes to Man? They could not have been man's ancestors, because they lived too recently. The best guess seems to be that they walked the Earth between 500,000 and a million years ago. The early men of Java and of China are older than that. So it looks as if the man-apes of South Africa were creatures which, like chimpanzees and other apes, descended from some common ancestor of Man and the apes.

Yet the man-apes were very different from other apes we know. For one thing, they walked upright. For another thing, it seems that they used tools. Both of these traits are so typically human that, by studying the man-apes, anthropologists hope to learn a great deal about how Man developed from his ape-like background.

Dr. Broom, after publishing his book, went back to looking for more fossils. At Sterkfontein he and his assistants uncovered a rare find — a perfectly preserved skull. Because it was very much like the Plesianthropus skull he had found earlier, he named this one Plesianthropus, too. But the new one was a female. Broom's assistants called her "Mrs. Ples."

In 1948 the diggers finally found something that proved beyond doubt that the South African man-apes walked erect. It was a complete pelvis. The pelvis of an ape is long and narrow. This one was shorter and wider. It also had a ball and socket arrangement for the hip bones. All this showed that the South African creature was a walker who could trudge comfortably for long distances. He *had* to be, to roam over the South African plains hunting for food. An ape, on the other hand, is not much of a walker. He can run much faster than a man, but he walks awkwardly.

But the most interesting question of all was the one about the man-ape's intelligence. True, he had only a small brain. Yet one thing suggested that he was more intelligent than other apes. That was the broken baboon skulls. The man-

80

ape must have used some kind of weapon, a stone or a club, to do that.

Led on by this clue, the scientific detectives hunted eagerly in South Africa for tools that the man-ape might have left in caves.

In 1947 a very promising discovery brought Dr. Dart back to digging. One of his students had been excavating a cave called Makapan. This cave had a kind of stone curtain over the entrance, formed by water trickling down from a cliff and washing down lime which hardened into limestone. It had made a wonderful home for animals, and later for men. In the high layers of the floor were old hand axes of Stone Age man. What excited Dr. Dart was that in deeper layers the student had found the fossil skull of a baboon such as lived in the man-apes' period.

Makapan Cave Where Prometheus Bones Were Found

Dart went to dig in this cave. To his great joy, he found some bones of man-apes and of baboons with cracked skulls. What was more, at the same level there was an accumulation of black charcoal. This must be the remains of wood fires. Did the man-apes know how to build fires? The charcoal was strong evidence that they did. What a discovery! If the man-apes used fire, they were closer to being human than anybody had thought.

Dart named the man-ape fossils in the cave Prometheus, after the Greek deity who gave fire to Man.

He hunted eagerly through the rock for some sign of weapons or tools. There was nothing that looked like a stone tool. But there were leg bones of antelopes — piles of them. Might the man-apes have used these as clubs? Indeed they might have. The ends of the antelope bones fitted perfectly the cracks in the baboons' skulls!

There were also long bones of horses and other animals. Some were broken into long splinters. These, too, Dart thought, might have been used as tools or weapons.

Many scientists again doubted Dart's conclusions. Scientists are always cautious about reading too much into new evidence. They have to consider other possible explanations. Maybe the charcoal came from accidental rubbish fires. The piles of animal bones might be just the leavings of food that hyenas, for instance, had dragged into the cave.

Dr. Dart looked into this last question. He investigated everything that was known about the habits of hyenas. And he finally announced that hyenas could *not* have been responsible for the collections of bones in the cave. Hyenas didn't collect food but ate dead animals in the field, usually the leavings of animals killed by other beasts. Besides, they had a habit of eating up the whole animal, bones and all.

Still, the question whether the man-apes used tools has not been finally settled. In some of their caves, diggers have

82

found pebbles which seem to have been brought there from river beds some distance away. Were these used as tools? The evidence is too indefinite to say.

What, then, can we say about the Australopithecines, as the South African man-apes are called?

If we came across an Australopithecine today, how would we treat him? Would we put him in a zoo, like a chimpanzee or other animal? Or would we treat him like a human being — a very dim-witted human being, to be sure, but a creature who could get along on his own in our world, after a fashion?

We can't decide such a question just by looking at his anatomy. The skull tells us that he had a small brain — less than half the size of modern man's brain. But that is not a complete answer to what he could do. To judge how human he was, we would have to see how he behaved in various situations.

How skillful and clever was he about finding food? How far did the mother go in caring for her young? How did the man-apes communicate among themselves, if at all? How did they fight? Their small canine teeth were not much good for fighting; did they battle with clubs? (Fighting with deadly superweapons seems to be a human invention.) How did they solve problems?

We don't yet have definite answers to any of these questions, and probably never will have. But we can deduce a few things about the man-ape's way of living.

He certainly could walk upright, very much like a man. Perhaps he was better at running than at walking, as all the apes are. He lived on a diet of small animals, roots, grubs, and a wide variety of other foods that he could catch or hunt down. He probably slept in the open and visited caves to hide or take shelter. It seems likely that he used some crude tools that he could pick up and did not have to make. He may

83

also have hunted and traveled about in groups, because life on the open plains would have been dangerous for him alone.

Without much doubt, Australopithecus fell short of being human in the most important way of all. He couldn't talk. We have to come to this conclusion from the small size of his brain and the structure of his jaw. According to all the signs, he simply didn't have the equipment for talking.

So Australopithecus was less than a man. Where, when, and how, then, did our ancestors step across the line between ape and Man?

Within the last few years, the fossil hunters have at last come upon a big clue. It seems to be the most exciting of them all. And this great discovery, too, turned up in Africa.

Cavemen Fighting Over Kill

84

Dr. Leakey

12

THE OLDEST MAN?

In Tanganyika, East Africa, is a valley called Olduvai Gorge. Long, long ago there was a lake in this place. Animals came to drink. Some of them died and left their bones on the edge of the lake. And then, over the course of time, their bones and the lake itself were buried under mud and sand washed over the site by flooding rains. Layer after layer piled up as one rainy period followed another. The layers hardened into strata of rock. The old lake bed was buried deep.

But about 100,000 years ago an earthquake made a crack right down the eastern side of Africa. This crack became the Great Rift Valley. After that, rains poured into the Great Rift through a side valley. That side valley became Olduvai Gorge. After thousands of years, the streams wore through the rock to the ancient lake bed itself. And in the steep sides of the gorge one could see the strata that had piled up. They looked like the layers of an enormous cake.

Serengeti Plain

Olduvai Gorge

Zinjanthropus skull here

Bajbal Depression

Mt. Malasin

Side Gorge

Ngorongoro Crater

Mt. Oldeani

Arusha →

Oldeani

Lake Eyasi

Lake Manyara

KENYA
UGANDA
Lake
Victoria
Nairobi
Lake
Eyasi
TANGANYIKA

In 1911 a German scientist named Kattwinkel discovered Olduvai Gorge. He was collecting specimens of insects in this wild region, and one day, while chasing a butterfly, he nearly fell into the gorge. Peering over the edge, Kattwinkel looked down into a chasm 300 feet deep. He forgot all about the butterfly he had lost. The exposed strata fascinated him. Quickly Kattwinkel made his way down to the bottom of the valley. He found the layer cake full of prizes. There were fossils all over the place!

Other German scientists made expeditions to the gorge. But in 1914 World War I stopped their explorations. Olduvai Gorge was left alone until 1931.

Then an English scientist named L. S. B. Leakey, who had been brought up in East Africa, went to visit the place. Living in East Africa, of course he had heard of Olduvai Gorge. He and his wife were both anthropologists. They thought that the old lake site should be a good place to hunt for early Man. Bodies of water have always been favorite camping sites for the human race. And here nature had conveniently excavated a very ancient lake where men might have lived hundreds of thousands of years ago.

Dr. Leakey was the son of missionaries in Kenya. He was born in a thatched hut among the Kikuyu tribe. When he was a baby, the elders of the tribe came to his hut to spit on him — a sign of respect. He grew up with the Kikuyu children and learned the tribal language. Later he was elected an elder of the tribe.

Even as a boy, Leakey began to collect Stone Age tools that could be found in the neighborhood. Then he went to England to study archaeology and anthropology at the University of Cambridge. He came back to Africa all ready to take up the search for early man.

Mary Leakey, his wife, had exactly the same interest. She, too, was a fine anthropologist. From her studies she had

86

decided that an island called Rusinga in Africa's Lake Victoria would be a good place to dig for fossils. How right she proved to be! So many fossil apes were found on this island that it came to be called the cradle of mankind. Mary Leakey started it all by turning up the first complete skull of a fossil ape of the Miocene period. At the time, there happened to be, in a London zoo, a popular chimpanzee named Consul. So her fossil was named *Proconsul*, meaning an ancestor of Consul.

In 1931, then, Dr. and Mrs. Leakey set off with high hopes for Olduvai Gorge. It was not an easy place to get to. There were no roads through the desert. They drove in a "land rover" — an English jeep. For seven days they bounced over bumps and rocks and shrubs, stirring up clouds of dust as they plowed on. They drove past herds of curious elephants and antelopes and zebras. Giraffes craned their long necks toward the car and then galloped away, swaying from side to side in their funny gait. Lions prowled around their camp at night. Hyenas and rhinoceroses came to call. The animals were attracted by the smell of water the Leakeys were carrying.

Water was a big problem at Olduvai. After the Leakeys got there, they found that during the dry season the nearest water was a spring 35 miles away from the old lake site. Every drop of water they used had to be carried the 35 miles.

It was a rocky, dusty place. Work here would be full of hardships. But as soon as the Leakeys took a look around in the gorge, they knew that they had an exciting life's work ahead of them. The valley was a fossil hunter's dream. Spread out on the cliff sides before them was a pageant of history.

They were sure that in the layers of the layer cake they would find a continuous story of the development of life and of Man, stretching over hundreds of thousands of years.

They started digging. In the deepest layer they found the remains of a dinotherium, the earliest known elephant,

Digging in Olduvai Gorge

which in Europe became extinct before the Pleistocene, more than a million years ago. They also dug up fossils of the middle Pleistocene — a giant pig the size of a rhinoceros, and a sheep six feet high at the shoulder.

In the same layer they came upon some broken pebbles. At first it looked as if they were merely pebbles that had been chipped by being knocked around. But when more and more of these peculiar chipped pebbles turned up, the Leakeys took a very close look at them. They then saw that the stones had been chipped in a certain special way. First a piece had been knocked off by a blow from the right, then another by a blow from the left, then a third by a blow from the right again. This treatment gave each pebble a rough cutting edge.

In other words, the pebbles had been formed into tools! And who else could have made them but a man?

Working on up into higher strata, the Leakeys found round stones which had been used as bolas. A bola is a stone tied at the end of a cord or vine; it is thrown at the legs of animals to catch them.

Still higher, the Leakeys found many stone hand-axes.

Pebble Tools

All this proved that what they had hoped for was true. Men *had* lived in this place, back to hundreds of thousands of years ago. If only they could find the bones of that very early man who had made the chipped-pebble tools!

The Leakeys decided to keep hunting for him. Year after year they went back to Olduvai Gorge. Each summer Dr. Leakey would take a seven weeks' leave from his job as director of the Nairobi Museum for their digging expedition. Seven weeks were all they could afford.

They took their children along. And the children were a big help in the digging. Their oldest son, Jonathan, found the jaw of a giant baboon; they named it for him — *Simopithecus jonathoni*. Their youngest son, Philip, made an astonishing discovery. They had been finding pieces of remarkably thick fossil eggshells. One day Philip dug up a leg bone of the bird that had laid these huge eggs. The bone was so big that it looked like the leg of a giraffe! The bird must have been more than twelve feet tall.

Summer after summer, the Leakey family stuck to its hard, hot, uncomfortable work. On their hands and knees they went over the rough ground inch by inch. The temperature often was 110 degrees.

At last, on July 17, 1959, it happened — the thing they had worked for all this time.

That morning Dr. Leakey had a headache. His wife ordered him to stay in bed and went off to search alone. She drove off in the land rover, taking along their two dogs, Toots and Sally. The dogs were important members of the team. They kept watch during the digging and gave warning of snakes, lions, and other visitors.

In a little while Dr. Leakey, lying in his tent, heard the land rover coming back. He heard his wife calling excitedly, "I've got him! I've got him!"

He jumped out of bed. "What happened? What have you got?"

Hunters with Bola

"Come quick!" she cried. "I've found our man! The one we've been looking for. I've found his teeth!"

Dr. Leakey forgot his headache. He jumped into the car, and together they rode as fast as they could to her find.

Mrs. Leakey had been going over the ground where they had first picked up the pebble tools in 1931. Suddenly she saw a piece of bone sticking out of a rock. Close by were two huge teeth in the rock. They were enormous, and they looked human!

When they got to the place, Dr. Leakey tumbled out of the car and inspected the teeth. They were human, all right. They were the largest human teeth he had ever seen.

The Leakeys were so happy they almost wept. After 28 years of work, they had found the ancient man of Olduvai Gorge at last.

They were impatient to dig the teeth out of the rock, but first there was another job to be done. The discovery had to be photographed *in situ* — in the place where it was found. So they called in a professional photographer. He arrived the next day and took pictures.

Then the Leakeys and their helpers went to work digging out the teeth and bones. With dental picks and camel-hair brushes they chipped away carefully in the rock and soil. They sifted through tons of rock and dust. And after 19 days, they had almost all of a human skull. It was broken into 400 pieces, from the pressures of centuries of contractions and expansions of the rock. But Dr. Leakey set to work putting the pieces of the skull together.

To get an idea of what this work is like, you might try smashing a teapot to smithereens, spading the pieces thoroughly

91

into the soil and stones in a hillside, and then finding all the pieces and putting them together in the original form.

This was what Dr. Leakey had to do, and he did it. When he got through, the skull was all there except the lower jaw.

He called the man *Zinjanthropus*, which means "man of East Africa" (Zinj is the Arabic word for Eastern Africa).

Zinjanthropus turned out to have a skull which was bigger than that of Australopithecus but smaller than that of modern man. The face looked human, though the forehead was very low. The most interesting thing about it was the teeth. The front teeth and the canines were small. This man could not possibly have used them for fighting or for skinning animals. The back teeth, however, were enormous. Probably they were used for chewing coarse vegetable food. Anyway, what the teeth showed was that an ordinary-sized man might have giant molars.

Zinjanthropus was about 18 years old when he died. The Leakeys knew this because he had his wisdom teeth, the last molars that come in the late teens, but he had not had them long, because they were not much worn. He had a bony ridge on top of his skull, which meant that he must have had powerful jaw muscles to match his big back teeth. This ridge is like the one on top of a gorilla's skull, but much smaller.

Zinjanthropus, with his low brow and small brain, could not have been very intelligent. Could he talk? It seems, from

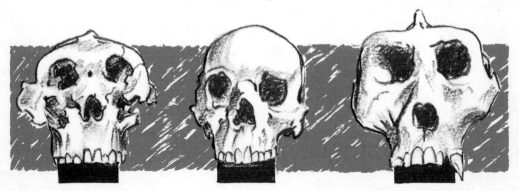

Skulls of Zinjanthropus, Modern Man, and Gorilla

the curve of his cheek bones, that he had tongue muscles attached to them. So he may have been able to speak.

Zinjanthropus was no beauty. But he was a man. His human teeth are one piece of evidence. But the most important evidence is the tools that were found with him.

Near the skull the Leakeys found many stone tools, which Zinjanthropus apparently had used for cutting meat and cracking bones. They dug up cracked bones, too. These were mostly from young animals. It seems that Zinjanthropus was not a very good hunter; he caught only young, weak game.

There were also more remains of Zinjanthropus himself. Two leg bones and pieces of another skeleton turned up. The Leakeys now were being helped with money to carry on their digging, so the work could go on all year instead of only during summer vacations.

One day in 1960 Dr. Leakey, at the Museum in Nairobi, got an excited call from the Olduvai camp over the radio.

"We have found a foot! Almost all the bones, including the heel and ankle bones."

"Is it Zinjanthropus?"

"No, it's from a lower level."

Dr. Leakey rushed out to the camp as fast as he could. Besides the foot, the diggers dug up some finger bones, a tooth, and some pieces of a skull and a lower jaw.

The creature to whom these bones had belonged had died a violent death. Its skull was fractured. The tooth showed that it was about twelve years old. Was it a human child? Dr. Leakey could not say for sure. At the same level they did find some very rough, simple, stone tools — simpler than the tools of Zinjanthropus.

There were many bones of tortoises and catfish around this older camp site. Perhaps the creatures who had lived there — human or near-human — were too clumsy to catch most animals and got their meat mainly by picking up turtles

Zinjanthropus

Watching Game at a Water Hole

on the lake shore and grabbing catfish with their hands in the shallow lake waters. They may also have eaten rats, mice, and lizards, for tiny bones of these animals also were found strewn about in the camp site.

What next? The Leakeys had found what they had started looking for. They were sure that they had traced man back to his earliest beginnings at Olduvai. Couldn't they stop now and take a rest? By no means. There was a lot more to see and find out. In the higher layers up the face of the gorge lay a great deal more of Man's history.

One mystery that led them on was the case of the human ancestor called Abbevillean or Chellean man. This was the man whose stone hand-axes had been found by Boucher de Perthes at Abbeville and at Chelles in France. No one had ever found the maker of the tools himself. There were no fossils of Chellean man. He was just a ghost-like creature known only from his tools. But now Dr. Leakey had dug up some hand-axes of the Chellean type in Olduvai Gorge. Furthermore, in 1954 he had found two enormous milk teeth with these tools. It seemed that they must be the teeth of Chellean man. And if teeth were there, wasn't there a good chance that the skull would turn up in Olduvai Gorge some day?

Through the years the Leakeys hunted and hunted for bones of Chellean man. In 1960, almost by accident, this search, too, ended in victory.

Working with a geologist who planned to make a map of Olduvai Gorge, Dr. Leakey one day climbed a hill to get a broad view of the diggings. For the first time he noticed an exposed layer which he had overlooked and not yet dug into. It was at the same level as the stratum in which he had found the Chellean tools.

The next morning Leakey went to this new layer and began to poke around in it. And there, in a bare little gully, he came upon some pieces of human skull.

FRANCE

Chelles

Chellean man at last! Dr. Leakey was so excited he could hardly speak. It was almost as thrilling a moment as when he had found Zinjanthropus. Here was a skull for which scientists had been searching more than a hundred years.

The skull turned out to be remarkable. It was big and heavy, with thick brow ridges. Its owner must have been a powerful man. That fitted in with the huge bola stones found in the Chellean deposits, and also with the fossils of giant pigs, giraffes, and sheep that lay in the same place. Chellean man must have been a match for those big animals.

This, for the time being, is the end of the story of Olduvai Gorge. But the gorge had one more big surprise, which is the subject of our next chapter.

Chellean Hand-Axe

96

Olduvai Gor

AFRICA

13

HOW OLD IS MAN?

According to every sign, Zinjanthropus was one of the earliest men that walked the Earth. But how old is he? How long has Man been in existence? When did he arise from his ape-like ancestors and begin to develop as a human being?

To answer that question, scientists first had to have some idea of how old the Earth itself is.

In 1650 Archbishop Ussher said that according to the Bible the world was no more than 6,000 years old.

A century later, after scientists began to realize that it was much older than that, Count Buffon estimated that the age of the Earth was about 100,000 years.

The Hindus long ago guessed that the Earth was a couple of million years old.

By the beginning of the twentieth century, geologists and other scientists had raised the estimate to 100 million years.

And how old was Man? Well, all the fossils of Man were found in rocks of the Pleistocene. This is the period of the Ice Ages. It was believed to cover the last million years. So Man was probably something less than one million years old.

Early in the twentieth century, scientists made a discovery that changed the time scale. They learned that they could measure the age of rocks by means of radioactivity.

We all know now that some of the substances in the earth are radioactive. This means that their atoms break down, giving off radiation and pieces of themselves which are called "nuclear particles." When an element breaks down in this way, it becomes another element. For instance, the element uranium, through radioactivity, gradually changes into lead.

A Core Cut Out of Ancient Strata for Measurement of The Ages of the Layers

The physicists were able to measure the rate at which each radioactive substance breaks down. In the case of uranium, it takes about four and a half billion years for half of the atoms to change to lead. This is called the "half-life" of uranium.

So scientists could tell the age of any given rock by measuring the amount of lead formed by the breakdown of uranium. In the same way, they could measure age by the decay of other radioactive substances. In other words, they used radioactive materials in the Earth as clocks to tell how much time had passed since they were formed originally.

And when the scientists consulted these clocks, they discovered that the Earth was not 100 million years but nearly *five billion* years old!

Some of the fossil plants in the oldest rocks turned out to be about a billion years old. The oldest animal fossils were about 500 million years. And the Cenozoic Era, the era of the primates, has lasted 69 million years. In short, it took our ancestors many, many millions of years to evolve into Man.

This still did not answer the question about how old the human race itself is.

When Dr. Leakey dug up Zinjanthropus, he announced that he estimated Zinjanthropus to be at least 600,000 years old. Privately he thought that Zinj was probably much older.

Leakey based his estimate mainly on the kinds of extinct animals that were found with Zinj. But this was not a very reliable way of measuring age. How could anybody be sure how old the animals were?

Luckily, Zinj happened to be lying right in an excellent radioactive clock. His bones were surrounded by volcanic rock. This volcanic material, boiling out of a volcano, must have been formed at about the time that Zinj lived. Maybe, by analyzing the material, experts might be able to tell how old it was.

Two geologists at the University of California, Jack F. Evernden and Garniss M. Curtis, decided to try. They tested many samples of the volcanic rock in which Zinjanthropus was buried. The clock they used was radioactive potassium 40. This decays into argon. So they measured the amount of argon in the rock.

What did they find? The rock was 1,750,000 years old!

A tremendous surprise. Zinjanthropus was three times older than Dr. Leakey had estimated.

When the two California scientists wrote to Dr. Leakey and announced their results in May, 1961, fossil hunters all over the world were astonished. If further investigations confirmed that Zinj was really nearly two million years old, the whole time scale of Man's life on the Earth would have to be looked at again.

But the fossil hunters were not disappointed by this news. In fact, they were inclined to cheer. The new age made much better sense. It had always been a puzzle to explain how Man had evolved so fast, when it took so long for the earlier animals to evolve into higher forms. How could Man have developed into such a complicated being as he is in a mere million years? Most animals evolved very slowly. It took the horse, for instance, about 30 million years to develop into its modern form.

Furthermore, the evolution from Man's ancestors to Man himself also took a very long time. In 1961 the Leakeys made a new discovery. In a farmer's fields in Kenya, not very far from Olduvai Gorge, they found pieces of skull and a lower tooth of an ancient creature which seemed midway between apes and Man. Drs. Evernden and Curtis measured its age as 14 million years! So it seems it took at least that long for our apelike ancestors to evolve into the first, primitive man.

Once Man emerged, however, he developed much more rapidly than other animals. Even early Man had one thing that set him apart: the ability to think. This speeded up his development enormously, as we shall see.

Time Scales of the Evolution of the Horse and Man

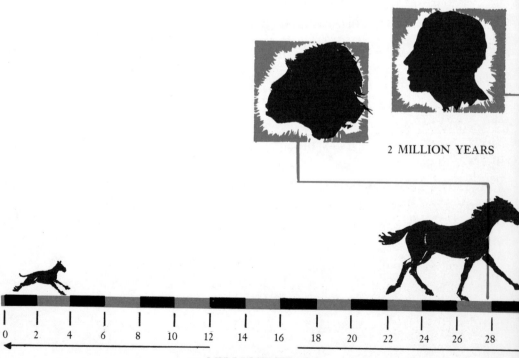

2 MILLION YEARS

0 2 4 6 8 10 12 14 16 18 20 22 24 26 28

30 MILLION YEARS

14

WHAT MADE MAN HUMAN?

The fossil detectives are closing in on the answer to the great mystery. True, they have not found any creature that they can call the missing link. They cannot point to any one fossil and say: "This was our ancestor." Instead they have found a whole menagerie of possible ancestors — advanced apes, man-apes, and various kinds of early men. But still, they are learning that there is, after all, one important link that led from the apes to Man.

This link can't be pinned down to any particular creature or any particular change in the body. The thing that turned an ape into Man was more subtle than that. It was a change in behavior.

The detectives' long search has finally led them to a discovery which in its way is more exciting than mere bones. Let us see what it is.

Look at an ape. At first glance it seems that he has all the basic things he needs to develop into a man. He has two excellent eyes set in the front of his head, so that his vision is as good as a man's. His eyes can see color, as most of the lower animals, such as the dog, cannot. He has hands which are able to grasp things. He has legs and feet on which he can stand up and run. (Running came before walking in the primate.) And the man-ape of South Africa, with his widened pelvis and erect posture, was even built so that he could walk long distances — which gave him a very important advantage in hunting for food.

Furthermore, the apes and the man-apes had a brain which was much better developed than that of the lower animals. The brain was still small, but it had the possibilities for growing bigger. It was on the way to becoming a human brain.

Why, then, did the apes and the man-apes remain just apes? Why, after all these hundreds of thousands of years, is the clever chimpanzee still no more than a chimpanzee? Why did the South African man-apes die off without ever becoming human?

Many years ago the fossil hunters thought they had found the answer. It was the use of tools, they said, that transformed apes into men. Our ancestors started on the road to manhood when they began to use tools.

But in recent years, scientists have learned that tool-using is not a talent that belongs only to Man. The South African man-apes, it seems, used pebbles and animal bones as weapons. As a matter of fact, many animals employ natural tools. Some birds dig insects out of the bark of a tree with a twig or thorn

Features in Which Apes and Man Differ from Other Animals —
Brain, Eyes, Pelvis, Hands, and Feet

102

that they hold in their beak. There is a certain wasp which, after laying its eggs, uses a small pebble to smooth the ground around them. Seagulls around New York have been known to crack clams by dropping them on parkways or the tops of cars. And a chimpanzee will use a stick to get a banana that is beyond its reach. In fact, it will go farther than that: if the stick is too short and a bamboo pole happens to be handy, the chimp will put the end of the stick into the hollow pole to make the pole long enough to reach!

No, it is not mere tool-using that separates Man from the apes. It is something more than that. And the anthropologists found their main clue in those broken pebbles of Zinjanthropus at Olduvai.

Zinj chipped those pebbles to make a sharper tool. In doing that, he was using foresight. He was not just picking up something that happened to be handy on the spur of the moment. A bird or an insect or a chimp might do that by instinct. But Zinj was beginning to think, to look ahead, to develop the use of his brain.

In short, tool-*making* was the step that started our ancestors on the road to manhood.

No doubt it all began when some primate, without thinking, impulsively picked up a stone and crushed an animal that would have got away. The discovery must have been as dramatic as Man's later invention of the wheel or even the airplane. All of a sudden our apish ancestor felt a new power. With the help of the stone, he had accomplished something he never could before.

The first time — maybe the first few times, until the lesson sank in — the use of the stone was an accident. But the habit grew, and the young, watching their parents wield stones, carried on the practice from generation to generation. Gradually they learned to throw stones and other missiles to catch animals. They learned to hack at game with a rock to get at

103

the meat. The South African man-apes even began deliberately to collect big pebbles from river banks and big bones from animals for use as weapons to bash baboons' skulls.

They never got beyond that. They didn't have the brain power to figure out that they could improve these implements or make tools of their own.

But somewhere some lucky primate did make that step. Again it was probably an accident. Trying to cut up an animal that he had killed for meat, he may have picked up a sharp-edged stone and discovered that it did a better job than a round, blunt stone. He may have noticed further that banging one stone against another caused the stone to break and gave it a cutting edge.

Whatever way it happened, Olduvai man took this great step forward. The remains at his lakeside camp show that he had learned how to chip pebbles to make a crude hand-axe.

Once that breakthrough into tool-making came about, all bars were down. Progress could begin to speed up, and go on without limit. The tools got better and better, and so did the brain. In fact, the tools and the brain advanced together, each influencing the other.

The new man no longer had to depend on his teeth to defend himself and to tear at his food. His teeth became finer, his snout smaller, and his face more vertical. He no longer had to swing through the trees to escape from his enemies; more and more he walked about and developed an upright posture. His hands were now free for handling and making things. They became better and better adapted to this purpose.

Gradually his whole body evolved to fit the needs of a tool-using creature. And the new life that the tools made possible also helped develop his brain.

In this new way of life, those who were most intelligent in using and inventing tools had the best chances of surviving and bringing up a family. They were more successful in getting food and defending themselves against enemies. They could

104

make clothing and shelters against cold, storms, and other dangers of their environment. They could change the environment instead of being at its mercy.

So Natural Selection now favored the men with the better brains. As time went on, the brain grew in size and power. The main new development was in the forward part of the brain where thinking is done — the cerebrum — and especially the roof of the cerebrum, called the cortex.

Now we can understand why Man developed so fast, and how he spread all over the world. During the great Ice Ages he was able to live in cold climates where the only other animals that survived were those with heavy coats of fur. Neanderthal and our other ancestors could do this because they had learned to live in caves and make fire. Man was beginning to make his own world.

The fossil detectives at last are beginning to put together the pieces of the puzzle and draw a picture of Man's early history. This is the picture as they see it now.

The story opens with our earliest human ancestors living like wild animals, getting along from day to day. They lived in the open, sometimes taking shelter in bad weather under a rock ledge or in the mouth of a cave. To have drinking water, they had to live near a lake or a stream. They fed on wild fruits, seeds, roots, nuts, lizards, mice, birds' eggs, insects, fish, turtles — any small prey they could easily pick up or catch. Occasionally they would make a meal on the carcass of a bigger animal that a lion or other powerful hunter had killed.

After they discovered how to make tools, they began to hunt and kill the bigger animals themselves. They became primarily meat-eaters. They discovered fire and learned to cook the meat, because it tasted better that way. They skinned animals to wear the fur as clothing.

Around their fires and camp sites, little settlements formed. Two or three or more families might band together and hunt

and cook as a group. But these bands never grew big. It was all they could do to find enough food for the dozen or so people who were living together. Besides, they couldn't communicate very well. If they had begun to talk at all, their language was meager — not much more than a collection of grunts and cries.

Without language, without time for anything but the constant hunt for food, the human race at first progressed very slowly. For hundreds of thousands of years, men got along with clubs and chipped pebbles. But gradually the tools were being refined. And then, suddenly, the story in the strata shows a burst of progress in tool-making.

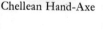

Chellean Hand-Axe

This shows up in deposits of maybe half a million years ago. One important new development was the hand-axe found at Chelles and Abbeville in France and at one of the levels in Olduvai Gorge. Compared with the earlier pebble tools, the Chellean hand-axe was very efficient. It could be used for many different jobs — chopping, cutting, scraping, digging, and so on. And with this tool, men could shape other tools of wood and bone.

From that point on, improvements in tool-making went faster. Men made better and better hand-axes. Some of these

Communal Life in Cave-Man Times

improved forms are called Acheulian, because they were first found near the town of St. Acheul in France. And besides the hand-axes, our ancestors by this time were making smaller, finer tools of flakes chipped from a stone.

A hand-axe of the Chellean or Acheulian type is called a "core" tool. This means that a piece of stone is chipped down to a "core" which is the finished, shaped tool. A "flake" tool, on the other hand, is made of a thin chip knocked off the stone.

In Europe the favorite stone for early man's tools was flint. This stone is a kind of quartz, often found in chalk deposits. It is an excellent stone to work with, because a chunk of fresh flint can be chipped neatly and easily.

Some of the late hand-axes show a lot of skill in stone-working. For instance, there is the Levalloisian hand-axe (named for the French town of Levallois, where archeologists dug it up). The makers of this tool first chipped a block of flint down to a core. Then, with one skillful blow, they split the core lengthwise. That gave them a flat axe-blade with a sharp edge, as you can see in the drawings on page 109.

People used to think that Stone Age man must have spent a lot of time making these tools. After all, without a regular job or games or newspapers or television to occupy his time, he had all the time in the world on his hands, didn't he? Don't believe it for a minute. He was kept busy from morning till night just hunting around for enough to eat. He couldn't afford to spend all day chipping stone. And we now have pretty good evidence that he didn't.

Dr. Leakey investigated this question. How long would it take to make a Stone Age tool? He sat down and tried making such tools himself. He was pleased to discover that with a little practice he could make them very quickly. He found, for instance, that by tapping all around the edge of a flint core with a hard object, he could get it to split into a Levalloisian hand-axe.

About 100,000 years ago, Neanderthal man appeared on the scene in Europe. What kinds of tools did he have? Well, we have some very good specimens. A lot of them were found in a cave in France called Moustier, so Neanderthal's tools are called Mousterian.

They are a good deal like the Levalloisian tools, but more carefully made. Neanderthal had learned to make not only hand-axes, scrapers, and other cutting tools but also spear heads. He probably attached these to wooden spear shafts, and it seems that he also made wooden handles for his scrapers.

By this time Man had become the king of the Earth. Neanderthal was more than a match for mammoths, bears, and all other beasts. He established himself in Europe, in the Far East, in Palestine, and in other places; skeletons of types of Neanderthals have been found in all these locations.

And then Neanderthal suddenly and mysteriously disappeared. We cannot tell why. Maybe his type was just swallowed up by interbreeding with more modern species of man. Or maybe the smarter species killed him off.

At any rate, the species to which we belong, *Homo sapiens*, finally made its appearance and took over the Earth.

108

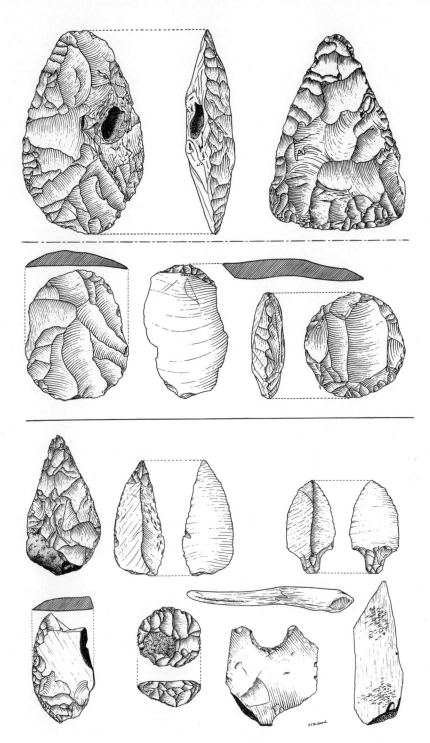

Three Types of Stone Tools: the Chellean *(top)*,
the Levalloisian *(middle)*, and the Mousterian
Tools of Neanderthal Man *(bottom)*

109

The first members of our species that we know about were the Cro-Magnon men, who lived in caves in France about 35,000 years ago. The tools they left behind are beautiful. They made flint knives, drills, and scrapers of various kinds. They also made chisels for working on bone and wood. Out of bone, ivory, and antlers they carved things for their clothes — needles, buttons, and buckles. There are lovely ivory figures in their caves which show the kinds of clothes they wore. Among their garments were trousers and shirts with fitted sleeves.

These were the people who made the beautiful cave paintings and sculptures that have been found in ancient caves of France and Spain.

The period of all the early tool-makers is called the Paleolithic, or Old Stone Age. Toward the end of this period men invented spear throwers, the bow and arrow, and the bow-drill for making fires. By this time they had little trouble catching plenty of game and fish. Life became easier. There was food enough for more people, and the human population began to multiply faster. It spread over the world everywhere except in America, where the first men apparently did not arrive until somewhere around 20,000 years ago.

About 20,000 years ago the fourth Ice Age began to pass away. The climate became milder. The glaciers melted and the seas rose. Lakes and rivers and forests and grassy plains took the place of the ice sheets in Europe, Asia, and North America. Many of the giant animals died off.

It was not so easy to catch the smaller, swifter game on which people now had to depend for food. But Man's brain carried him through. He was able to adjust to the new conditions. He became a more expert hunter and made better tools.

A wonderful collection of these tools has been found in an old peat bog in Denmark. They show something new — small, fine points and blades called "microliths." These were used as arrowheads and set into handles of bone or wood to

make knives, drills, and other cutting tools. We call them Maglemosian, from the Danish word *maglemose*, which means a bog or swamp.

Because the Maglemosian tools lay under water and were not exposed to the air, even those made of bone and wood are beautifully preserved. There were polished axes and clubs, canoe paddles, sled runners, bows and arrows, fish hooks, harpoons, and even fish nets.

Man was moving forward to a new period — the Neolithic, or New Stone Age. He ate fish and shellfish, hunted deer and small forest animals, shot birds, and also gathered wild grains and other vegetable foods. And then, somewhere around 9,000 years ago, he made the biggest step of all.

He graduated from hunting to farming.

By that time people had come to know quite a bit about plants and animals. Now they discovered that they could plant seeds and raise some of the wild plants that they had used for food. They found that they could tame animals such as the dog, the sheep, and the goat. So little groups of people began to practice agriculture. Archeologists have found remains of some of the earliest farming settlements in Iraq, in Iran, and at Jericho in Palestine.

Why was Man's graduation from a hunter to a farmer so important? Well, it isn't hard to see what tremendous changes this would bring about in his way of life. His supply of food suddenly jumped. He could store away reserve supplies of grain and other food products. Instead of everybody spending all his time hunting for food, some people could be freed for other jobs. They could spin and weave cloth, build houses, make pottery, carve, paint, and create a written language.

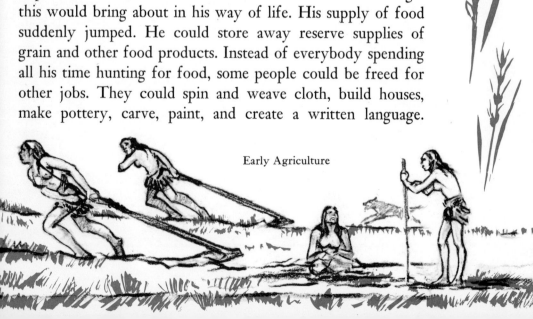

Early Agriculture

What was most important, they could settle down and build villages, towns, and cities.

In short, civilization was born. The human race came closer together and worked together. People developed the arts of communication and shared their knowledge. Man's life steadily became more exciting. Century after century, Man created a new world of wonders.

We do not need to dig up fossils to tell us what has happened in the last few thousand years. Most of that story is written in books. And in that short time Man has accomplished vastly more than in all the millions of years of his lonely struggles in the wilderness.

We started out on a search for our lost ancestors. Every step of the search has been an adventure. And now that we look back on the whole long story, we can see how lucky we are to be here in the most exciting century of all, looking forward to the greater wonders that Man is sure to perform in the times ahead. Let us hope that he does not blow up the world but continues to move on, as he has in the past, to new discoveries and a better life.

FOR FURTHER READING

Roy C. Andrews, *Meet Your Ancestors*. New York, Viking Press, 1945.

Gerald Ames and Rose Wyler, *The First People in the World*. New York, Harper & Brothers, 1958.

William A. Burns, *Man and His Tools*. New York, Whittlesey House, 1956.

W. E. LeGros Clark, *History of the Primates*. Chicago, Phoenix Books, 1957.

Raymond A. Dart and Dennis Craig, *Adventures with the Missing Link*. New York, Harper & Brothers, 1959.

May Edel, *Story of Our Ancestors*. Boston, Little, Brown and Company, 1955.

Carroll L. Fenton, *Prehistoric World: The Story of Animal Life in Past Ages*. New York, John Day, 1954.

Raymond Holden, *Secrets in the Dust: The Story of Archaeology*. New York, Dodd, Mead and Company, 1960.

William W. Howells, *Mankind in the Making: The Story of Human Evolution*. New York, Doubleday and Company, 1959.

Robert L. Lehrman, *The Long Road to Man*. New York, Basic Books, 1961.

Ruth Moore, *Man, Time, and Fossils: The Story of Evolution*. New York, Alfred A. Knopf, 1953.

Kenneth P. Oakley, *Man the Tool-Maker*. London, British Museum, 1950.

G. H. B. and Marjorie Quennell, *Everyday Life in Prehistoric Times*. New York, G. P. Putnam's Sons, 1959.

William E. Scheele, *Prehistoric Man and the Primates*. Cleveland, World Publishing Company, 1957.

Millicent Selsam, *Voyage of the Beagle*. New York, Harper & Brothers, 1960.

G. H. R. Von Koenigswald, *Meeting Prehistoric Man*. New York, Harper & Brothers, 1957.

Franz Weidenreich, *Apes, Giants, and Man*. Chicago, University of Chicago Press, 1946.

Anne T. White, *The First Men in the World*. New York, Random House, 1953.

GLOSSARY

ABBEVILLIAN   A prehistoric culture named for stone tools found at Abbeville on the Somme River in France.

ACHEULIAN   A type of stone tools found first in the cave of St. Acheul in France and later in other places.

AMPHIBIANS   Animals that live on land but lay their eggs in water; their young live in the water until they mature.

ARCHEAN   The name of the oldest known rocks and the era of the earth up to about 500 million years ago.

AUSTRALOPITHECUS   A genus (group) of ancient man-apes whose fossils have been found in South Africa.

BRECCIA   A rock composed of broken pieces cemented together. Bone breccia contains pieces of fossil bone.

CENOZOIC   The era of recent life. This is the geological era from about 70 million years ago to the present time.

CHELLEAN   A type of stone tools found at Chelles on the Seine River in France. It is like the Abbevillian.

FORAMEN MAGNUM   The opening in the base of the skull through which the spinal cord connects to the brain.

FOSSIL   Any remains of an animal or plant of past geological ages preserved in the earth.

GEOLOGY   The science of the history of the earth and its life, as shown in the rocks.

HOMO SAPIENS   The name of the modern species of man. *Homo* is the Latin word for man, and *sapiens* means "wise."

IN SITU   In place. In archaeology this usually refers to the place where a fossil was found.

INVERTEBRATE   Any animal without a backbone.

LEVALLOISIAN   A type of stone tools found at Levallois in France. These resemble Neanderthal man's tools.

114

MAGLEMOSIAN   The name given to tools and other man-made articles found in peat-bogs, dating back to the Mesolithic Age of man. (Maglemose is the Danish word for swamp.)

MESOLITHIC   The Middle Stone Age of man. It is the period between the Paleolithic and the Neolithic ages.

MESOZOIC   The era of middle life. It came before the Cenozoic and lasted from about 195 to 70 million years ago.

MOUSTERIAN   Tools and other remains of Neanderthal man, named from the cave of Le Moustier in France.

NEANDERTHAL   One of the races of early man, named for the valley in Germany where his remains were first found.

NEOLITHIC   The New Stone Age of man, which began late in the Pleistocene period.

PALEOLITHIC   The Old Stone Age of man; the first half of the Pleistocene.

PALEONTOLOGY   The science of the life of past geological ages, based on the study of fossils.

PALEOZOIC   The era of ancient life, from the time of the oldest fossils, about 500 million to 200 million years ago.

PELVIS   The bony arch that supports the hind legs of vertebrates.

PLEISTOCENE   The geological period that began one or two million years ago and spanned the Ice Ages.

PITHECANTHROPUS   Primitive types of men found in Java and China. The word means "ape man."

PRIMATES   The order of mammals consisting of man, apes, monkeys, and monkey-like creatures.

SPECIES   A particular type of animal or plant. *Homo sapiens,* Neanderthal, and *Pithecanthropus erectus* are species of men.

VERTEBRATES   Animals with backbones, from the fishes to man.

ZINJANTHROPUS   Man of East Africa. One of the earliest types of true man.

INDEX

116

All of the photographs were supplied through the courtesy of the American Museum of Natural History except the following:

page 21: The Bettmann Archive
55: The China Medical Board
65: Fritz Goro
81: Harper & Brothers
(From *Adventures with the Missing Link* by
Dr. Raymond A. Dart with Dennis Craig.
Copyright © 1959 Raymond A. Dart
Reprinted by permission of Harper & Brothers)